GLASTONBURY—
HER SAINTS
A.D. 37—1539

Glastonbury, "The Mother of Saints."—

HER SAINTS

A.D. 37—1539.

BY THE

Revd. Lionel Smithett Lewis, M.A.,
Vicar of Glastonbury.

Author of "St. Joseph of Arimathea at Glastonbury; or, the Apostolic Church of Britain."

SECOND AND ENLARGED EDITION.

Containing (*inter alia*) :—

1. A Foreword in answer to the Dean of Wells.

2. Accounts of two Saints not before linked up with Glastonbury— St. Thecla of Germany and St. Siegfrid of Norway.

RESEARCH INTO LOST KNOWLEDGE
ORGANISATION

c/o R.I.L.K.O. Books,

RILKO BOOKS
10 CHURCH STREET
STEEPLE BUMPSTEAD
HAVERHILL, SUFFOLK
CB9 7DG
TEL: 01440 730901
FAX: 01440 730088

THOD

First published 1925
This Edition 1985

British Library Cataloguing in Publication Data

Lewis, Lionel Smithett
  Glastonbury — the mother of saints : her saints,
  A.D. 37-1539.
  1. Christian saints—England—Glastonbury
  (Somerset)—Legends—History and criticism
  I. Title
  398'.352   GR142.G5

  ISBN 0-902103-11-3

Printed and bound in Great Britain

With grateful thanks to Miss Grace Dazell-Walton.

PREFACE TO THE FIRST EDITION.

This story is long over-due. Would that some one more fitting had written it! I am only fitted by my love of the place and its wondrous story. It had to be done. So I have done it. As you have not done it, do not be too hard on one who has at least tried with the minimum of time at his disposal. I launch it into the world, and if it be read in the spirit in which it is written, it must do some good.

September 11th, 1925.

———

PREFACE TO THE SECOND EDITION.

When the First Edition of this book appeared, the Press was good enough to foretell a second. I should be sorry to disappoint them. So here it is.

LIONEL S. LEWIS.

The Vicarage, Glastonbury.
November 11th, 1927.

CONTENTS.

Research into Lost Knowledge Organisation is pleased and proud to republish "GLASTONBURY — The Mother of Saints — HER SAINTS" by the Rev. Lionel Smithett Lewis, M.A. The book has been out of print for too long and we feel it will be welcomed as a companion to his well loved work on St. Joseph of Aramathea.

Elizabeth Leader,
Founder Member, R.I.L.K.O.

FOREWORD TO THE SECOND EDITION.

SOME ANSWER TO THE DEAN OF WELLS'S "TWO GLASTONBURY LEGENDS."

In the 1st Edition of this book I expressed the hope that Dr. Armitage Robinson, Dean of Wells, would have his gifts kindled in defence of early Glastonbury traditions. Since that edition the Dean has written a book. The Dean of Wells was formerly Dean of Westminster, between both of which places and Glastonbury there has been an age-long rivalry. The double mantle has proved too much for him. His book is called " Two Glastonbury Legends." In it he tries to destroy the age-long associ-ation of St. Joseph of Arimathea and King Arthur with Glastonbury.

Before I say a few words about the Dean's effort I might add that Mr. Christopher Hollis, a recent convert to Rome, has written another book, the religious purpose of which is manifest, called " Glastonbury and England." Mr. Hollis mentally accepts the whole position of the Dean. He is a Wellensian. Having accepted the Dean's findings with his mind as a matter of course, his whole soul revolts from it, and he relieves himself by amusing tirades against "the Dons" and their attitude to Glaston-bury. It is not an inspiring sight—a man suffering simultaneously from mental acquiescence and spiritual indigestion. Let us look away to the Dean, who is wrapped in calm without a doubt.

Lest anyone should take these two books too seriously I pen these few lines. It is obviously impossible to deal fully in a foreword with the Dean's attitude. For the sake of brevity I am going to omit what he says about the tradition of King Arthur. I commend to the reader my suggestion, at the end of my article on King Arthur in the text of this book, that after the discovery of Arthur's tomb in Henry II's reign, Glastonbury's two Celtic stories of St. Joseph and King Arthur, long forgotten through the Saxon and Norman Conquests, were carried by the Troubadours through Europe. Hence their inextricable interweaving in the lays of the Holy Grail.

Even to touch lightly upon the Dean's treatment of
the St. Joseph tradition one must go back to his 1921
essay on "The Antiquity of Glastonbury." In this book
he lays down the law as to what passages have been
inserted in the original of William of Malmesbury's "The
Antiquity of Glastonbury," not because of anachronisms,
save here and there, nor upon the evidence of a different
hand-writing. Such evidence we can accept. The Dean
starts with the theory that the monks "took over the
legend of Joseph of Arimathea and the Holy Grail,"[1] and
tries to make everything fit into this theory. In his later
book he writes about an "early tradition" on this subject,
and deliberately charges the monks with *appropriating*[2] it.
And this without a shred of positive evidence. It is at
the end of our horizon that we reign with an infinite might.
In the absence of anything to contradict us we can let
ourselves go (and when a new fact comes in view we can
save our faces by posing as discoverers). The Dean
simply begs the question and wastes much time and
ingenuity. He takes much pains to disjoint that which
naturally fits together. *Cui bono?* Even the absence of
earlier evidence is no proof that there never was any.

It should be remembered that William of Malmesbury
(who visited many Abbeys and became an adopted monk
and Precentor of Glastonbury) wrote his 1st edition of
"The Acts of the Bishops and "The Acts of the Kings"
about 1125, and his 2nd and 3rd editions between 1138
and 1140. Then, coming to Glastonbury at the invitation
of the monks, reading its charters and its ancient books,
living in its traditions, and seeing its pilgrimages, he
wrote his "Antiquity of Glastonbury" between 1129 and
1139. And the Dean himself expresses the view that the
latter edition of the "Acts of the Kings" and the
"Antiquity of Glastonbury" were being written about the
same time at Glastonbury itself. In other words, William
was correcting an earlier book and writing a new one
while daily adding to his knowledge. It is much easier
and safer to write entirely fresh than to adapt old material.
Here is the very soil for great likenesses, corrections and
slight differences. But the Dean assumes that the portion
referring to Glastonbury in the last edition of the "Acts
of the Kings" and the account of the same period in the
"Antiquity of Glastonbury" were identically the same, and
that any differences in the latter were later interpolations.
And this although one book is a history of English Kings,

[1] Somerset Historical Essays, p. 1.
[2] Two Glastonbury Legends, p. 39.

which just has a reference to Glastonbury, and the other
an actual history of Glastonbury itself. Surely it is more
natural to think that when William came to write " The
Antiquity of Glastonbury " he took as his text what he
had written in " The Acts of the Kings," and, as greater
knowledge and certainty came to him, made some alter-
ations for the last edition of the latter, and still greater
ones for his new book all about Glastonbury. I would
urge that if you put the two accounts side by side, without
the Dean's pre-supposition, you will find nothing really
contradictory, but only development and greater knowledge adapted and narrated. One is sure, quite uncon-
sciously, the Dean's treatment of the two passages is more
than biassed—misleading. One knows that there are
naturally some interpolations in the text. But the Dean's
evidence as to the stories of St. Joseph and King Arthur
being deliberate appropriations leaves one quite cold.

Having said this I am going to place side by side
the only passages from the two books which the Dean
treats in that fair way. And I think that any unbiassed
mind will think that the same hand (William of Malmesbury's) wrote the two passages as they stand, and that.
seeing the circumstances under which they were written,
they exhibit just the little differences which we might
expect to find.

I print the Dean's italics.

ACTS OF THE KINGS.	THE ANTIQUITY OF GLASTONBURY.
(1st Edition 1125, 3rd Edition between 1129 and 1139).	(1st Edition between 1129 and 1139).
There came therefore by the sending of Eleutherius preachers to Britain, *the effect of whose work will last for ever, though their names have perished through the long neglect of time.*	There came therefore by the sending of Eleutherius (as) preachers to Britain, *these two most holy men, Phagan and Deruvian, even as it is declared in the Charter of St. Patrick and the Deeds of the Britons.*

[The Dean calls this " at the outset a notable discrepancy." The date of the 3rd edition of " The Acts
of the Kings " is not certain. In any case, William
might have neglected to add to the 3rd edition of one
book what he wrote fresh in the 1st edition of the other.
He gives his authorities for his new statements—(1) The
Charter of St. Patrick, which he saw at Glastonbury ; (2)
Geoffrey of Monmouth's " Deeds of the Britons." We
know that William and Geoffrey were contemporaries, and
both dedicated their books to Robert, Duke of Gloucester,
and so very possibly conversed with or corresponded with

one another. It is just the sort of piece of local personal information which we should expect to see in a book about Glastonbury. Yet the Dean calls it "a notable discrepancy" instead of a natural addition. I will complete the passages side by side.]

The work of these men therefore was the Old Church of St. Mary in Glastonbury, as antiquity has not failed faithfully to hand down through the ages of the past. There is also that written evidence of good credit found in certain places to this effect: The Church of Glastonbury did none other men's hands make, but actual disciples of Christ built it.

Nor is this irreconcilable with truth; for if the Apostle Philip preached to the Gauls, as Freculfus says in the fourth chapter of his second book, it may be believed that he cast the seeds of his doctrine across the sea as well. *But lest I should seem to cheat the expectations of my readers by fanciful opinions, I will leave disputable matters and gird myself to the narration of solid facts.*

The Church of which we speak
. . . .

By the work of these men, therefore was the Old Church of St. Mary in Glastonbury *restored,* as antiquity has not failed faithfully to hand down through the ages of the past. There is also that written evidence of good credit found *at St. Edmunds* to this effect: The Church of Glastonbury did none other men's hands make, but actual disciples of Christ built it; *being sent, to wit by St. Philip the Apostle, as was said above.*

Nor is this irreconcilable with truth; for if the Apostle Philip preached to the Gauls, as Freculphus says in the fourth chapter of his second book, it may be believed that he cast the seeds of his doctrine across the sea as well.

[Here follows a story of a monk of St. Denys, a legend about the island of Glastonbury, and a discussion of the meaning of its various names.]

The Church of which *indeed* we speak . . . .

Anyone can see that *both* books contain distinct reference (1) to the tradition *that the disciples of Christ built the Old Church at Glastonbury;* (2) that somehow St. Philip had something to do with it; (3) that later Eleutherius's missionaries did much for the Old Church (The language of the *"Acts of the Kings"* at first suggests that they built it, but this is corrected *later in the same passage* by the statement that "actual disciples of Christ built it. The *"Antiquity of Glastonbury"* says plainly that their work was restoration, affirms that the disciples of Christ built it, and adds that these disciples were sent by St. Philip, pointing back to the story that St. Joseph and others were sent by St. Philip). It is all quite clear. Before he went to Glastonbury William had heard certain stories that he was not quite sure of. He went, and was convinced that they were true. But the Dean considers the greater details in the book all about Glastonbury as "a later invention foisted into the original work."

I have dealt at some length on the Dean's conclusions

in his earlier essay on "The Antiquity of Glastonbury" in his "Somerset Historical Essays, 1921," because these are the conclusions that made him approach the "Two Glastonbury Legends" as forgeries and inventions.

In his book "Two Glastonbury Legends" the Dean hopelessly muddles up two quite separate Glastonbury traditions, and thinks one a variation of the other.[1] Glastonbury has the world-known tradition that St. Joseph brought the Holy Grail, the cup used at the Last Supper, and that it was buried by him in Chalice Hill, near Chalice Well, their very names being derived from the story. Melchinus or Maelgwynn of Llandaff in the 5th century tells us that St. Joseph brought with him two phials, one containing the blood and one the sweat of Our Lord, which were buried with him in the Old Church. These are perfectly distinct traditions. The Dean failed to see for himself, as he might have done, that in the 15th century they were regarded as distinct legends. There is a coat of arms, consisting of a cross between two cruets. For over a century this has been considered a canting-rebus of Abbot Richard Bere, because, among other Abbey insignia that were put on Abbey buildings, he was fond of using this one. It is popularly said to be a cross between two beer-jugs. I came to reject this belief, and was convinced that the two "beer-jugs" were the two cruets buried with St. Joseph. To my great joy in 1923 I found confirmation of my belief. In 15th century glass in the south window of the Sanctuary of Glastonbury Parish Church I found the shield with drops of sweat in the background. The first person whom I shewed it to was Mr. Bligh Bond, who had also independently arrived at the same conclusion as to the "beer-jugs." The second was the Dean of Wells. The Dean of Wells, in his book, refers to this shield in the window. Unfortunately he neither came to see it again nor wrote to me to refresh his memory. He speaks of drops of blood in the background, when it should have been drops of sweat. (He also calls it 16th century glass). But the great point is that he has failed to notice the important thing. Within a golden bordure on the top of this shield is a most interesting depiction of the Holy Grail itself. An Eastern story says that the cup used at the Last Supper was shaped out of one ruby and was brought from heaven by an angel. Here in this glass is the Holy Grail, blood red as a ruby, shaped like the Mystic Rose of Glastonbury, inverted, and two rays of light proceeding from it towards the shield. Here, within a foot of glass, is the enshrining of Glaston-

[1] He even goes so far as to call one a "counter-tradition" which "directly excludes" the other! (p. 39).

bury's three sacred legends, linking her with St. Joseph
and Our Lord—the Holy Grail the Two Cruets, and the
Mystic Rose which grew from one drop of the Sang Réal.
So in the 15th century, at any rate, the two first traditions
were regarded as quite distinct. The Dean's cleverness
makes him prone to neglect the obvious in pursuit of the
abstruse. He not only wrongly described and failed to
notice details in this glass, but in his list of representations
of St. Joseph with the two cruets he neither sought nor
enquired whether it was to be found in the natural place,
Glastonbury. He omitted the figure over the west door
in Glastonbury's own Parish Church! However, we can
forgive these little things. But it is too much when it
comes to throwing doubt on the age-long belief of St.
Joseph's burial at Glastonbury on the flimsiest evidence.
All sense of proportion is lost when he puts such emphasis
on the recollections of William Goode, who served in the
Old Church as a child of eight, and was only twelve years
old at the time of the Dissolution of the Monastery, and
died in exile abroad. From this child's recollections (told
in after years) of some nameless monk's or monks' conversation, he says that the monks generally were not sure
whether St. Joseph was buried at Glastonbury or no! And
yet the Dean himself has to record Maelgwyn's, John
of Glastonbury's and William of Worcester's records,
Edward III's writ in 1345 to search for the body at
Glastonbury Abbey, and an East Anglian chronicler's
statement in 1367, " the bodies of Joseph of Arimathea
and his companions were found at Glastonbury." Glastonbury's whole story, all her place names, all her legends,
are redolent of St. Joseph. But the recollection of a
conversation heard as a child, by a man who is an
unknown quantity, after years of exile and the shock of
the Dissolution, outweighs the tradition and history of
centuries! It is absurdly out of proportion.

The Dean is so anxious to destroy the beautiful
tradition of St. Joseph. But he fails to account for someone founding the most ancient and flourishing British
branch of the Church. Whom does he suggest as a
substitute? Nature abhors a vacuum, and it is a futile
crime to try and make one. Historians of the highest
repute hail Glastonbury as the Mother Church of Britain.
The St. Joseph tradition supplies the cause. William of
Malmesbury (*pace* the Dean), Archbishop Ussher, Sir
Henry Spelman, Parsons the Jesuit, Polydore Vergil, *inter
alia*, are constructive historians whose positive teachings
will remain when the negative portion of the Dean's are

forgotten. If Tertullian (b. A.D. 155) wrote that "regions of Britain which never have been penetrated by the Roman arms have received the religion of Christ"; if Origen (b. A.D. 185) said that "the divine goodness of Our Lord and Saviour is equally diffused among the Britons, the Africans, and other nations of the world"; if Eusebius (b. A.D. 260) hands down that "the apostles passed beyond the ocean to the isles called the Britannic Isles"; if Gildas, the first British historian (b. A.D. 516), who died at Glastonbury, tells us that "Christ the True Sun afforded His light, the knowledge of His precepts, to our island in the last year as we know of Tiberius Caesar," i.e., A.D. 37—somebody brought it. If the Dean attacks the ancient and consistent story of St. Joseph it is his duty to try and offer some other explanation.

If, as we know, St. Hilary, St. Athanasius, St. Chrysostom, St. Jerome and St. Augustine of Hippo all applaud the vigour, soundness and extent of the British Church in the 4th century; if that Church had a hecatomb of martyrs in the Diocletian persecution in A.D. 300; if British Bishops were present at the Councils of Arles in A.D. 314, Nicaea in 325, Sardica in 347, and Ariminium in 359; if there are venerable corroborative traditions that the British Beatus died in the Switzerland which he converted in A.D. 96, and Mansuetus, a British companion of St. Clement was martyred in A.D. 110 after converting Loraine and Illyria; if our fellow countryman, Marcellus, laid down his life in A.D. 166 after founding the Archbishopric of Tréves; if St. Cadval founded the Cathedral of Tarentum in Italy in A.D. 170; if Mello (b. A.D. 256) became the British Bishop of Rouen, and the Word flowed from Britain to Ireland and thence to Scotland in the 5th century—then there was a great and flourishing British Church in the earliest days, and it is up to the Dean to give some other evidence of its origin before he attempts on bare suspicion to demolish the treasured belief that Glastonbury was the Mother of it and St. Joseph the Founder.

The Dean is very learned, and his books are always intensely interesting and mines of information. But, after all, the important point is—is he altogether a safe guide? Many gifted people are not. We have said something about his "Two Glastonbury Legends." Let us take two other things: (1) The notices in Glastonbury Abbey, he being Chairman of the Executive Committee of its Trustees; (2) A slab in his own Cathedral. To be a great scholar on any subject one must necessarily have one's limitations. It is very easy to be so occupied in bending over a MS. as to forget all the evidence of the world around. And it is possible to be meticulously careful about dots to i's and extraordinarily oblivious to ordinary every-day facts.

First, let us take the descriptive notices which the Executive Committee have at last been persuaded to put up at the Abbey, giving some idea of what the buildings are.

(*a*) In July, 1921, the Dean very properly ordered an excavation to find the site of St. David's pillar, put up some 1,400 years ago. He followed the directions of an ancient metal inscription formerly on a pillar of the Abbey, giving an account of the coming of St. Joseph and others. It said that the column was erected by St. David for the express purpose of keeping in memory which was the Old Church. It gave, amongst other things, the exact distance from the centre of the east end of the Old Wattle Church to the centre of this column set up to the north of it. The excavators measured that distance exactly. They dug and came straight down upon the foundations of this column, which are still exposed. And yet the following is the wretched, colourless notice put up for visitors :—

" SITE OF COLUMN SET UP TO INDICATE THE EASTERN LIMIT OF THE ORIGINAL CHURCH OF WATTLES."

Not a suggestion that it claimed to be St. David's 1,400-year-old column, put up expressly by him " lest the site or size of the church should be forgotten through additions." No hint of how it had been discovered ! No visitor unlearned in the story could have any idea of the interest of this excavation and the claims of this spot. So tremulously, meticulously careful ! And yet—

(*b*) The same mind responsible for this notice, and so ready to demolish age-long beliefs, is guilty, as Chairman of the Committee at least, of allowing in the Abbey buildings the following new notice, which starts an absolutely groundless myth in the minds of unsuspecting visitors. The Dean forgets that some future historian may think his evidence at least as valuable as he thinks William Goode's. One of the most barbarous things ever done at Glastonbury was done not long before the Reformation for the sake of filthy lucre. People were paying so highly to be buried in the Old Church that the holy dead were disturbed, a crypt dug out, and the floor of the ancient church raised. This 15th century crypt ran right under St. Joseph's Chapel and under the Galilee (which connected the chapel with the nave), and a shrine to

St. Joseph appears to have been made at the east end
of it. A most amazing notice now appears at the east
end of the crypt :—

> "POSSIBLE SITE OF ALTAR OF ST. JOSEPH
> OF ARIMATHEA."

Unsuspecting visitors stand thrilled, believing that they
are standing before the site of the altar erected by St.
Joseph, before which he, St. Patrick, St. David, St. Gildas
and others were said to be buried. And those who know
the personnel of the Committee, but do not know much
of the building, believe that they have the authority of
this careful scholar, the Dean, for the statement ; whereas
the site of the altar erected by St. Joseph must have been
in the chapel above, many feet to the westward ! For the
crypt did not exist till some fourteen centuries later ! The
notice had not been up three months before two F.S.A.'s
wrote to me in distress, asking me whatever it meant.
Of course, the Dean knows. And, of course, he never
meant to convey such a wrong impression. But a guide
who lays sacrilegious hands on venerable traditions, and
is so tremulously afraid of stating the triumphant vindi-
cation by excavation of an ancient inscription, should at
least be careful not to start new myths by unguarded
wording of notices.

Next, let us consider a notice in Wells Cathedral. A
good many years ago I stood aglow in the nave there.
Before me on the floor was a slab with these words :—

> "INA REX, 688-726."

"Here then," I thought, "lies Ina of the wonderful
laws and the mighty sword ! Ina the devout ! Is there
any other Cathedral that can add to the tombs of Saxon
Bishops the burial place of so early a Saxon King ?" But
Ina was buried in Rome ! What did it mean ? Later a
verger told me that the Dean thought that somewhere
about there Ina probably built a church ! Now I am told
that some fifteen years ago an old stone with the same
inscription was perishing, and the Dean ordered this new
one to take its place. I am also told that an old stone
coffin was found underneath, and even that the Cathedral
annals claim that Ina was buried in the nave. Which is
it ? Construction is worthier of a great scholar than
destruction. To add to the glories of Wells is greater
than to disparage Glastonbury. Can he, dare he, challenge
the story that Ina lies buried at Rome? If so, let him
do so. It would be splendid. If not, why perpetuate
a crumbling slab, which must inevitably convey a totally

wrong impression? What a lost opportunity! The painful carefulness shewn over the St. David's column notice would have been in place. The rashness of this notice and that about the Altar of St. Joseph are akin. Strange that one so afraid to state or accept ancient traditions should be so careless about starting or approving new myths!

This little enquiry into the grounds of the Dean's condemnation of our legends, and as to whether, with all his great learning, he is really altogether a safe guide, may bring comfort to lovers of Glastonbury and its lore.[1]

After all, must we take the Dean too seriously?

There are interludes when scholars look up from their books and take a glimpse of the world around. "Two Glastonbury Legends," on its last page,[2] has this passage :

> "Yet they (the legends) claim respectful treatment on very various grounds. He who rejects them as unworthy trivialities, and will have nothing but the unclothed skeleton of historically attested fact, cuts out the poetry from life and renders himself incapable of understanding the fulness of his inheritance."

This is exactly what the Dean has done. In that sentence the Dean has hanged himself. There he will hang—a man who wrote a book to assassinate two beautiful legends, but does not like to be called an assassin. This is probably the connecting link between him and his humble follower, Mr. Hollis. One commits the crime and the other is an accessory, but their subconscious minds know all the time it is a crime, and they are ashamed of it. It is all very pitiful. So much labour! So much ingenuity! I repeat *"Cui bono?"* If one can accept the St. Joseph story everything fits in like a jig-saw puzzle. No forcing is necessary. If not, nothing fits in. And people write books which their better selves condemn. It is an interesting psychological study.

---

[1] They will recall, as the Dean himself has had to admit, that the disputes of England, France and Spain as to precedence at the great Church Councils of Pisa, 1409, Constance, 1417, Sienna, 1424, and Basle, 1434, were decided in favour of England by Glastonbury's story, because St. Joseph brought the faith to England immediately after the Passion of Christ (" statim post passionem Jesu Christi"). Spain and France and the Councils generally must have had convincing proof, even if that proof no longer exists after the destruction of Glastonbury's great library and muniment room.

[2] p. 50.

Glastonbury, "The Mother of Saints."— HER SAINTS.

FIRST EPOCH.

ST. JOSEPH OF ARIMATHEA,

DIED AT GLASTONBURY, A.D. 82.

WHO has not heard that the earliest traditions and the place names of Glastonbury centre round St. Joseph of Arimathea? The tradition of St. Joseph coming and founding the Christian Church here fits in extraordinarily with tradition of other places and with history.

Eusebius (A.D. 260-340), Bishop of Cæsarea, and the Father of Church History after the sacred Canon closed, says : " The Apostles passed beyond the ocean to the isles called the Britannic Isles." Here is very early general corroborative evidence from the Eastern Church of the founding of the British Church in the Apostolic Age. And the primitive silence of the Eastern and Roman Churches as to the post-scripture history of St. Joseph is most significant. His coming to Britain and founding a Church here would account for it. Much of Britain at this time was outside the Roman Empire. For two hundred years from B.C.59, when Julius Cæsar made his first attempt to conquer her, not only was Britain fighting desperately against Rome, but so successfully that during that period every celebrated Roman general fought in Britain. And the Roman Church was too much taken up with her own troubles to think much about what was happening in other contemporary Churches, especially in outlandish parts. This silence about so important a person as St. Joseph is otherwise most strange. The one "honourable councillor" who had the courage to defend Christ in the Council ! One of only two men who had the devotion to claim His dead body when all seemed lost ! The story of St. Joseph at Glastonbury seems to explain everything.

Gildas, the British historian (A.D. 516-570), says: "Meanwhile these islands . . . received the beams of light, that is, the Holy precepts of Christ, the true Sun . . . at the latter part, as we know, of the reign of Tiberius Cæsar."[1] Those words of Gildas, "as we know," are peculiarly interesting, being a clear reference to a generally accepted knowledge, which is striking evidence from a native son of our native Church, who was its earliest historian. Nor should we forget that it is claimed that he lived many years at Glastonbury, and is buried there.[2]

This date, "the latter part of the reign of Tiberius," would be at the latest A.D. 37, four years after the Crucifixion. How well this fits in with the decisions of the Councils of Pisa, Constance, Sienna, and Basle, that the British Bishops took precedence of the French and Spanish, because our Church was founded immediately after the Passion of Christ!—"Statim post passionem Christi."[3]

An ancient MS., ascribed to Maelgwyn of Llandaff, said to be the uncle of St. David, which would be about A.D. 450, tells of St. Joseph's burial in St. Mary's Chapel (the ancient wattle Church), at Glastonbury, names the site of his grave (to the south of the altar), and says that he has with him two vessels, one with the Blood, and the other with the Sweat of Our Lord.[4]

The celebrated Vatican librarian, Cardinal Baronius, found an ancient MS. in the Vatican which tells of St. Joseph, Lazarus, Mary, Martha, and others being put into an open boat without oars or sails on the Levant, and floating down to, and landing, at Marseilles in A.D. 35.[5] This fits in with the Marseilles traditions of the settling there of Lazarus and his sisters, with which that city is saturated. It must be remembered that histories were few and far between, and that very many even of these have been lost. But tradition flourished in the winter nights over the fireside.

Then there is a tradition in the tin trade that St. Joseph was a metal merchant.[6] This would mean that he or his servants must have come to Britain to get tin for bronze. This, too, would account for his wealth. Tradition says that he went to Cornwall for tin, and the Somerset hills for

---

[1] Gildas. Sec. 8.
[2] V. pp. 42-43.
[3] " Disputatio super Dignitatem Angliæ et Galliæ in Concilio Constantiano." Theodore Martin, Lovar, 1571. These Councils were held respectively in 1409, 1417, 1424 and 1434.
[4] V. the Author's " St. Joseph of Arimathea at Glastonbury " (3rd Edn.), p. 25.
[5] V. ditto, p. 24.
[6] V. ditto, p, 17, and v. later pp. 73-75.

other metals.¹   In that case he may have been known as a
trader to the celebrated British King Arviragus, and to
Glastonbury before he came here as a Missionary.²

This brings us to the story of Glastonbury's greatest
historian, William of Malmesbury, who was the most
critical and accurate of early English historians.   He wrote
the *"Antiquities of Glastonbury"* about A.D. 1135, at the
invitation of the Monks of Glastonbury, after he had written
a history of the Kings of the English, and another of the
Bishops of the English, some ten years before.   There are
some obvious additions to his book on Glastonbury as it
has reached us.   But it is of interest to compare what he
wrote about Glastonbury in this book, and what he wrote in
the earlier book, the History of the Kings.   One sees new
phases in his knowledge and his convictions.   This critical
and truth-loving historian staying at the Abbey, seeing with
his eyes the evidence in stone, in processions of pilgrims,
and in worship, for men's beliefs, reading the ancient MSS.
and books of this once perhaps greatest of British libraries,
and drinking in with his ears the traditions of the shrine,
and comparing them with the claims of other religious
houses, wrote a reasoned and careful history of the place,
marking off very clearly certain chapters in its history.

He reminds us that in the persecution, when St.
Stephen was slain, all the disciples except the apostles
were scattered from Jerusalem.   This fits in with the date
of St. Joseph and the family at Bethany being placed in the
boat.   And who more likely to awaken the animosity of the
Jews ?   William quotes Freculphus, Bishop of Lisieux in the
ninth century, as having recorded that St. Philip the
Apostle went to France to preach.   He then adds that St.
Philip sent twelve men from France (to which the Vatican
MS. traced St. Joseph), to convert Britain, of whom St.
Joseph of Arimathea, St. Philip's " dearest friend," was
leader.   He gives the date as A.D. 63.   The different date
need not upset us.   We must expect differences of detail in
these ancient stories.

¹ There must be something distinctive about Mendip or British
metal. At Ostia, the sea-port of Rome, there was found not long ago
an ancient Roman drain-pipe below the chariot-road. It was a particularly good specimen and was bonded in some special way with tin.
Professor Russell Forbes cut off a section and sent it home to England
without comment for analysis. The verdict was that the metal came
from Mendip mines.

² Diodorus Siculus, writing just before Christ, traces the route of the
tin merchants from Marseilles to Cornwall. There is a traditional route
from the tin mines of Cornwall to the lead mines of the Mendips in
Somerset, some traces of which perhaps exist. V. Taylor's " The
Coming of the Saints," pp. 178-180.

He records that the great King Arviragus remained
unconverted, but that he was kind to the missionaries and
that three kings, Arviragus, and afterwards his son Marius,
and later Coel (who is buried at Glastonbury), Marius'
successor, between them granted them twelve hides of
land.[1]   It was probably as a sign that Arviragus had given
the land that St. Joseph planted his staff, which tradition
says grew into the Holy Thorn, an object of pilgrimage and
veneration all down the middle ages.   Arviragus' grant was
the beginning of the famous " Twelve Hides of Glaston,"
which is the name of a territorial hundred to this day.   The
Twelve Hides enormously expanded beyond twelve actual
hides.   It is worth noting that 1,000 years later, in that
great tax-book, Domesday Book, it is recorded that these
twelve hides had never paid tax.   Part of the hides given
by Arviragus himself was " Ynnis Witrin," an ancient
Celtic name for Glastonbury meaning probably the Crystal
Isle, "an island surrounded by thickets, woods and
marshes."   William tells us that they were warned by St.
Gabriel to build a church in honour of the Blessed Virgin
Mary, which they did of twisted twigs.   This is the
celebrated Wattle Church, " The Ecclesia Vetusta," " The
Olde Church," St. Joseph's Chapel, probably the first
above-ground Church in the world, the Mother Church of
Britain.   All down the ages it has been esteemed the most
sacred spot in Britain.   William cites " written evidence
of good credit found at St. Edmund's to this effect : The
Church of Glastonbury did none other men's hands make,
but actual disciples of Christ built it, being sent by St.
Philip the Apostle, as was said before." [2]   He further tells
us : " Thereupon the twelve Saints—so often mentioned—
paying devout homage in that same spot to God and the
Blessed Virgin, spending the time in vigils, fasts, and
prayers, were constantly sustained . . .   The said
Saints continued to live in the same hermitage for many
years, and were at last liberated from the prison of the
flesh.   The place then began to be a covert for wild beasts
—the spot which had before been the habitation of Saints—
until the Blessed Virgin was pleased to recall her House
of Prayer to the memory of the faithful." [3]

All the geography and folk lore of Glastonbury speak
of St. Joseph.   To the south-west of the town stands
Weary-all Hill, the ancient Wirral, the hill where he and

---

[1] William of Malmesbury's De Antiquitate, Cap. 1 and 33.   Lomax'
translation is used throughout.
[2] De Antiquitate, Cap. 2.
[3] De Antiquitate, Cap. 1.

his companions are said to have landed. The name was too
tempting not to be converted in the course of ages to
Weary-all, to denote the condition of the tired travellers.
The sea came up to it in those days. What are now some
seventeen miles of marshes were then awash. As recently
as Stuart days a tidal wave reached St. Benignus' Church
in the lower part of the town. Standing on the Tor Hill
on a moonlight night, with the valley bathed in mists, you
can get a very clear and beautiful picture of how the island
stood out of the water in those distant days. And a less
beautiful scene in the daylight when the floods are out also
helps one to understand. But it does not absolutely translate one as the moon and the mist do with only the help of
a very little imagination. Then one might be living at the
moment. And the sight of St. Joseph with his staff and
his companions would seem fitting. That staff that became
the world-famed Holy Thorn that blossoms at Christmas !
Although the original tree was destroyed by a fanatical
Puritan, who paid the penalty of his deed,[1] and although the
shoots cannot be struck, ere the venerable tree followed its
persecutor to the grave, loving hands budded and grafted
it, and its descendants are with us to-day, a Levantine
Thorn, hailing from the same land as St. Joseph, which
has never ceased to flower at Christmas, and gives us its
sweet flowers in the spring as well. Practically never without leaf, from October till May with buds on its boughs, it
bears an immemorial ever-present testimony to the story
of St. Joseph. The site of the present Vicarage was
chosen because the oldest and finest existing specimen of
the Holy Thorn of Glaston stood in what was enclosed as
its garden. There are less good trees in the Abbey ground,
and in the Churchyard. And even in America and the
Colonies they are growing. Then at the foot of the Tor,
that tower-crowned hill which dominates Somerset, and
can be seen from the borders of Devon and Gloucestershire,
is another almost eternal thing that speaks of St. Joseph—
the Chalice Well. Its name commemorates what he
brought from the Holy Land. More than 2,000 years ago
it was a sacred well of the Druids, before it became a sacred
Christian well, before the worship of the Sun had ceased on
the commanding hill, and a Church of the Crucified (alas,
now in ruins), proclaimed Christ from its summit. Pure
and limpid it pours its waters forth. Within the memory
of man they have never failed. They are as sure as the
secret of its source is uncertain. That secret it has kept

[1] V. the Author's " St. Joseph of Arimathea at Glastonbury " (3rd
Edn.), pp. 11-12.

all down the ages.   But when all the skill of modern science
fails, without a change of countenance it simply and
naturally steps in and supplies man's need, rivers of living
water that never fail, a type of what St. Joseph brought,
when he and his companions came and lived within its
spell.[1]

Cressy, the Benedictine Monk and Historian, who was
versed in the traditions of the great Benedictine Monastery
of Glastonbury, which were treasured among the Continental
Benedictine houses, tells us that St. Joseph of Arimathea
died at Glastonbury on July 27th, A.D. 82.   Once he had
hewn out of the living rock at some cost a far away tomb
for himself.   But the Christ came into his life, and that
tomb.   And the " honourable councillor," the rich man,
rose from his dead self, and died a russet-clad hermit, and
was buried in a wicker Church in far-off Britain.

ST. ARISTOBULUS.[2]

BURIED AT GLASTONBURY A.D. 99.

The name of Aristobulus, the companion and fellow-
worker of St. Paul, is associated with Glastonbury.   Though,
alas, owing to the flood of heathendom which temporarily
swamped the greater part of this country after the first
few centuries, the fact has been too much forgotten by
our Church, there is steady testimony from the Eastern
Church that St. Aristobulus was the first Bishop of the
Britons.   St. Dorotheus, Bishop of Tyre, A.D. 303, wrote :
" Aristobulus, whom Paul saluted, writing to the Romans,
was Bishop of Britain." [3]   Haleca, Bishop of Augusta, said,
" The memory of many martyrs is celebrated by the Britons,
especially that of St. Aristobulus, one of the seventy
disciples." [4]   And the same fact is more fully recorded in
the Martyrologies of the Greek Church.   The Greek
Menology for 15th March reads thus :   " Aristobulus was
one of the seventy disciples, and a follower of St. Paul
the Apostle, along with whom he preached the Gospel to
the whole world, and ministered to him.   He was chosen
by St. Paul to be the missionary bishop to the land of Britain,
inhabited by a very warlike and fierce race.   By them he
was often scourged, and repeatedly dragged as a criminal

---

[1] Unfailingly it yields 20,000 gallons a day, Miss A. M. Buckton,
its owner, says.

[2] V. the Author's " St. Joseph of Arimathea at Glastonbury " (3rd
Edn.), pp. 7, 10, 28-30 and 32.

[3] Synopsis de Apostol : Synops 23 " Aristobulus."

[4] Halecae Fragmenta in Martyr.

through their towns. Yet he converted many of them to
Christianity. He was there martyred after he had built
Churches and ordained deacons and priests for the island."
Hippolytus (early part of the third century) in his
list mentioned Aristobulus as "Bishop of the British."
Nor was the fact forgotten by our sister Church of
France. St. Ado, Archbishop of Vienne, A.D. 800-
874, says: "Natal day of Aristobulus, Bishop of Britain,
brother of St. Barnabas the Apostle, by whom he was
ordained Bishop. He was sent to Britain, where after
preaching the truth of Christ, and forming a Church, he
received martyrdom." [1] And amid the lore of the ancient
British Church, there remains to us the same story. "There
came with Bran the Blessed from Rome to Britain Arwystli
Hen" [2]—Aristobulus the Aged. This would not be later
than A.D. 58, for Bran the Aged, ex-Druid and ex-King,
and his son Caractacus, were taken prisoners to Rome in
A.D. 51. Caractacus stayed there about seven years. But
Bran is said to have come home first.

Let us sum up. There is reason to believe that St.
Paul lived in, and was martyred from the house of the
British princes at Rome.[3] And, as we have seen, the Greek
Martyrology tells us that it was St. Paul who chose
Aristobulus to be Missionary Bishop to Britain. St. Ado,
telling us that he was ordained by his own brother, St.
Barnabas, St. Paul's great comrade, also adds that he was
sent to Britain. St. Paul, writing to the Romans, greets
the household of Aristobulus, but not Aristobulus. He was
probably absent in Britain. And in the ancient British
Triads he is described as a "man of Italy." In the Silurian
List he is called Confessor or Instructor to Bran. And we
know that Beatus, the noble British missionary who converted Switzerland, and died A.D. 96 at Unterseen, on
Lake Thun, where his cell is still shown, was not only a
companion of Aristobulus, but, according to tradition, was
converted and baptized in Britain by St. Barnabas,[4] who,
St. Ado says, was Aristobulus' brother. According to this,

[1] Adonis Martyrologia, under March 17th.
[2] Achau Saint Prydain (Genealogies of the Saints of Britain).
[3] For the relation of the British Royal Family to Christianity and
St. Paul, see Bishop Burgess' "Origin of the Ancient British Church,"
pp. 21-54, 77-83, and 108-120; Conybeare and Howson's "Life and
Epistles of St. Paul," Vol. II, pp. 581-2, and 594-5; Archbishop Ussher's
Brit. Eccl. Antiq., p. 19; Archdeacon Williams' Claudia and Pudens;
R. W. Morgan's "St. Paul in Britain," pp. 195-6 and 211-2; and the
Author's "St. Joseph of Arimathea at Glastonbury," pp. 9-11.
       Theatr. Magnae Brit., Lib. VI, p. 9.
[4] V. the Author's "St. Joseph of Arimathea at Glastonbury,"
pp. 10, 29, 32.

St. Barnabas was here too. Possibly he came over with
St. Paul at an earlier period. And then, later, the giant,
caged himself in body but free in mind and soul, sent his
companion's brother to water and develop the seed sown,
and go still further afield. It is hard to think that among
the " Apostles " who " passed beyond the Ocean to the
Isles called the Britannic Isles " was not that chiefest who
promised to go " to the utmost bounds of the West," and
whom tradition perpetually associates with Britain. One
would like to think that he did really preach on that hill
where the great Cathedral dedicated to him has stood for
at any rate thirteen centuries, and that the people came up
to him from the sea-going fishing village round the ancient
Tower on the White Hill, and from Cheap-side, the
immemorially busy Mart of the Shopmen or Cheapmen, and
that he also preached under the oak that thenceforth bore
the name of Gospel Oak.[1] The agonies of ravages that our
country passed through, followed by an obedience that
would only recall what was pleasing and exalting to Rome,
wiped out so much of our early history. But here and there
like a rock above the sea traditions survive. And linking
them together with here and there the written word, we get
hints of the submerged continent beneath.

Not only St. Paul himself, but St. Barnabas, St. Simon
Zelotes, St. Aristobulus, and Joseph of Arimathea probably
actually trod our Britain. And of those there are distinct
traditions that St. Joseph and St. Aristobulus died at
Glastonbury itself. For Cressy, the Benedictine recorder of
Benedictine lore, tells us that Aristobulus, our first Christian
Bishop, alas, so forgotten on our shores in spite of wide and
long record from Eastern, Gallican and British Churches,
died at Glastonbury in A.D. 99. For a moment it may
startle us to hear that he died as a martyr, and yet died
at Christian Glastonbury. But the presence of a Christian
Church does not make the surrounding country Christian.
Britain was not yet converted. Avalon itself was still the
home of Druidism. The two religions were side by side.
Not till A.D. 167, our records tell us, did Christianity
prevail. And centuries later St. Indract was slain on a
pilgrimage a few miles from Glastonbury.[2] Like Arthur
later, Aristobulus may have come here to die of his wounds
and to sleep in a forgotten grave.

---

[1] The fact that there were various Gospel Oaks connected with
religious processions makes no difference. An oak with such a history
would be likely to be chosen for such a purpose.
[2] V. p. 19.

SECOND EPOCH.

SAINTS FAGAN & DYFAN.

We now come to an event, A.D. 166, in which tradition and records agree. After the religion brought here by St. Joseph and his companions had been quietly leavening the country for about one hundred years, suddenly Druidism fell with a crash. The first step was taken by a British King, who seeing Druidism and Christianity side by side, desired his people to be Christian, and sent to Rome for missionaries. There are people who think that the whole of this episode was invented so that Rome should appear to have some finger in the pie of the original conversion of Britain. Seeing how encroaching are her claims, and how her children have absorbed them, this suspicion may be pardoned. But against that we have a consensus of evidence by historians. There is undoubted evidence of a precedent Christianity in this country. All records state that the move came not from Rome but from Britain. Imperial Rome was the Mistress of the World, and the centre of civilisation. And as the simple story of these missionaries unrolls itself, there are traces of a very natural and inevitable precedent intercourse between the two countries.

Almost certainly members of the British Royal Family returned from their Roman captivity converted. Bran had been converted before. Quite certainly intercourse with Christian Romans and the Continent had been aiding in other portions of the Kingdom. There is a consensus of opinion that Lleiver Mawr (good King Lucius), great grand-son of Caractacus, and son and successor to King Coel, deliberately sent for missionaries to instruct his people, and there is a general agreement that it was Pope Eleutherius who was sent to. The date assigned is A.D. 166, and Eleutherius was not Pope till A.D. 176-7. It is extraordinarily unreasonable not to expect to find difficulties and discrepancies in such ancient history. Mistakes are eternally easy. Mistakes are sometimes only apparent. And our own knowledge to aid us in interpreting is so small. There may be a slip in dates. Or it may be that Eleutherius was appealed to, or deputed, to see to the matter before he was Pope. Either Gaul, our friendly neighbour Church, or Rome, the Mistress of the World, the centre of culture, where tradition says that Caractacus was converted,[1] was the natural place to send to. And Eleutherius may well have been the person who when Pope, or before he was Pope, had the matter in hand. But all histories attribute the initial move to Lucius.

Fagan and Dyfan, both Celts, were the names of the missionaries sent. Geoffrey of Monmouth tells us that Gildas, A.D. 516-570, recorded their names and acts in a book now lost, " *The Victory of Aurelius Ambrosius.*" [2] The second revision of the Liber Pontificalis about A.D. 685 has the story. Except for this the Venerable Bede, A.D. 673-735, is the earliest writer whose work is still extant who mentions Lucius and his appeal to Eleutherius.[3] This mention by Bede is enthrallingly interesting. Writing in his northern monastery of Jarrow, where he knew little or nothing of Glastonbury, which he does not mention, he yet tells us of the appeal to Eleutherius. The Anglo-Saxon *Chronicle* also gives it to us, and as is well known, the earlier part of that chronicle is written in archaic Anglo-Saxon, and may go back to the days of the Heptarchy. Geoffrey of Monmouth, in his History of the Britons, claims to be translating a most ancient Celtic MS. It was dedicated to Robert, Duke of Gloucester, who died in A.D. 1147, and in it he calls the missionaries Faganus and Duvanus, and tells of their wonderful success, and of the baptism of Lucius and his people,[4] and how the seats of the Druids became Bishoprics, and those of the Archdruids, Archbishoprics.[5] In A.D. 1135 William of Malmesbury wrote his great book on Glastonbury, and he tells us all about Lucius sending to Eleutherius. He calls the missionaries Phagan and Deruvian. Varying Latinisation of a Celtic name is just what we may be prepared for. The Welsh Triads, one at least of which was written in or before the sixth century.[6] give us the names of four missionaries, Dyfan and Fagan, Medwy and Elfan, all British names.[7] The Latin book of Llandaff, John of Teignmouth in his life of St. Dubricius,

<hr>

[1] For details about the British Royal Family and Christianity v. the Author's " St. Joseph of Arimathea at Glastonbury," pp. 9-13.
[2] History of the Britons, Bk. IV, C. 20.
[3] Bede's Ecclesiastical History, Bk. I, C. 4.
[4] Traditionally in the Chalice Well. He and his court are also said to have bathed in the baths below it, spoilt some 150 years ago by being turned into a small spa.
[5] V. History of the Britons, Bk. IV, Cap. 19 and 20.
[6] It names Glastonbury, Llan Iltud, and Ambresbury as the Three Perpetual Choirs of Britain. But Ambresbury ceased to be in the 6th Century.
[7] V. the Author's " St. Joseph of Arimathea at Glastonbury," pp. 13-5.

A.D. 1346, Capgrave, A.D. 1393-1464, and Archbishop
Ussher (De Brittanicarum Ecclesiarum Primordiis, pp.
49-50), tell us that Medwy and Elfan were the Britons sent
as emissaries to Eleutherius, and that they returned with
Dyfan and Fagan. The two latter were apparently, from
their names, Christian Britons. Nothing could have been
wiser than to have chosen such.

A great debt is owing to these much forgotten Saints.
They appear to have put the finishing touch to the conversion of Britain. William of Malmesbury, writing about
Glastonbury, tells us certain local details, linking them on
with the twelve Anchorites under St. Joseph of Arimathea, that "there, God leading them, they found an old
Church built, as 'twas said, by the hands of Christ's
disciples," and, "finding the house of prayer thus, were
transported with ineffable joy, and there remained returning
thanks to God for quite a long time, namely, for nine years";
that they found "the whole story in ancient writings" of
the coming of St. Joseph and his companions, and the giving
of the twelve hides of land ; that "they loved this spot above
all others, and they also, in memory of the first twelve,
chose twelve of their own, and made them live on the said
island with the approval of King Lucius. These twelve
thereafter abode there in divers spots as anchorites—in the
same spots, indeed, which the first twelve inhabited.[1] Yet
they used to meet together continuously in the Old Church
in order to celebrate Divine worship more devoutly. . .
And thus many succeeding these—but always twelve in
number—abode in the island many years up to the coming
of St. Patrick, the Apostle of the Irish.[2] Thus we arrive
at this. Gildas is said to have written of the coming of
these Saints in a book now lost. Bede, Geoffrey,[3] William,
and later writers all say that Lucius sent of his own will for
further teachers, and that he was baptized.

It is interesting to record that Cressy, the learned
Benedictine monk, who knew the traditions of the Benedictine Monastery of Glastonbury, some of which still linger
in Benedictine monasteries on the Continent, tells us in
his Church History of Brittany that King Lucius, accom-

[1] Traditionally in a dell just above the Chalice Well.
[2] De Antiquitate, Cap. 2.
[3] People with more impatience than imagination loftily reject
Geoffrey of Monmouth's wonderful history as pure fiction. Those who
accepted it all as quite accurate and gospel truth would try the patience
of even the imaginative. But the scornful rejectors might ask themselves the question why in view of the hatred and contempt between
the Norman, the Saxon, and the Briton, a Norman monk should forge
a history glorifying the Briton. And they might reflect, e.g., how in
general outline the British pedigrees support Geoffrey of Monmouth.

panied by his sister S. Emerita, finally went as a missionary through Bavaria, Rhoetia and Vindelicia, and was martyred near Curia in Germany. At Chur (Coire) the capital of the Grison canton, Switzerland, there is a very interesting old Cathedral where many relics remain. There they tell that in the crypt Lucius King of the British and his sister lie buried. These little confirmations surviving in foreign lands are of real interest. The fact that there was also a Lucius King of Edessa, and that there happened to be a place in Edessa called Britium, which is such a joy to many critics, leaves us quite cold. Why not? There is very little known of either Christian King except that they bore this quite common name.

There may be discrepancies and differences in these ancient versions of still older stories. But it is easier to believe such are inevitable than to think that the whole thing is a fiction. Supposing the gist of so ancient a story was true, would one not expect to find among writings so varied, and so distant in date from each other, differing details, dates, and names, and added colouring, unless one held a theory of verbatim inspiration? Is not this attitude more charitable and more intelligent than the fiction theory? This epoch of the second set of twelve Anchorites, their ranks constantly filled and lasting nearly three hundred years, is the second phase in the history of Christian Glastonbury.

THIRD EPOCH.

ST. PATRICK OF IRELAND.

We now come to the third great epoch. In my next claim for Glastonbury I shall raise nearly the whole Irish nation against me. One can conceive nothing else which could bring about an united Ireland. But I shall contemplate that miraculous spectacle with equanimity, believing that the weight of evidence is on my side. It is claimed that St. Patrick of Ireland returned to his native Britain, and spent his last years, and sleeps, at Glastonbury as its first Abbot. The modern Irish dispute this claim, and say he is buried in Ireland, but cannot agree where, naming Downpatrick, Saul, and Armagh! That a great Irish St. Patrick ushered in the third and last stage of Glastonbury's greatness, started the great Abbey, ruled it, and died there, seems undoubted. And unless there really were, as has been stated, three contemporary great Irish Patricks, Palla-

dius Patrick sent by the Pope Celestine to Ireland in A.D.
431, Succat Patrick the great Apostle of the Irish, who went
in A.D. 432 (?), and Senn Patrick (Old Patrick), the head
of St. Patrick's wise elders, who could be mistaken for each
other, which seems improbable, the evidence as a whole
compels us to think that the great St. Patrick lies at
Glastonbury. As a rule, when people are driven to think
that they see three similar people instead of one, their
vision and understanding are not working well, and they are
not safe guides.

St. Patrick's real name was Succat. He was a Briton,
and of noble birth, the name Patrick or Patricius simply
meaning "gentleman" or "nobleman" as late as the
seventh century. His father Calpurnius was a deacon and a
decurio, or magistrate. The same word is used of St.
Joseph of Arimathea, the honourable counsellor (nobilis
decurio) in Maelgwyn's MS.[1] His grandfather was Potitus,
a priest. A marginal note in the MS. of William of
Malmesbury's De Antiquitate by a later hand states that
St. Patrick's mother was "Conches, the sister of St.
Martin, Archbishop of Tours, as Martin testifieth in his
chronicle, ' St. Patrick.' " His birthplace was Bannavem
Taberniae (perhaps Bannavemta Berniae, or could it per-
haps even be Bonaventa Berniae, or Hiberniae, the latter
suggesting some dog Latin idea of easy access to Ireland ?).[2]
In what part of Britain this lies is a matter of speculation.
These few facts we learn from his own "Confession,"
written in very rude Latin revealing Irish idioms. There
are several MS. versions of it, with considerable variations.
The Book of Armagh, about A.D. 807, contains one copy.
Its author complains of the MS. being scarcely legible then.
This may account for variations in copies made by different
hands at different periods, especially as the style of them
is all the same, whatever the additions or omissions. St.
Patrick calls himself "indoctus et rusticissimus."[3]

[1] V. p. 2.
[2] Can it have been Bonavon or Bonafon, an ancient harbour near
Bonchurch, Isle of Wight? As regards my suggestion of Bona Venta
Hiberniae, there were several Ventas in Britain : Venta Vitgarom,
Venta of the Belgae (i.e., Winchester), Venta Slurum, Venta of the
Silures (i.e., Caerwent), Venta Cenonum, Venta of the Iceni (i.e.,
Caistor, near Norwich). Professor Haverfield, in "The Roman
Occupation of Britain," p. 193, says : "The exact sense of Venta is
unfortunately obscure. Perhaps the best explanation is that it means
a market centre or gathering-place for the surrounding country." His
editor, George Macdonald, adds a footnote rejecting the derivation of
Venta from the Celtic "gwent," a clearing, and says that Dr. Whitley
Stokes suggested to Professor Haverfield that the name might possibly
be connected with the Latin "vendere" and mean a market town
or business centre. He compared the Spanish "Venta," a wayside inn.
Ibid. p. 194.
[3] Unlearned and very rustic.

When he was about sixteen the Irish made a raid upon his neighbourhood, and carried him away as a slave. He had to tend cattle for six years. There, like the Prodigal Son, he came to himself. Let him speak for himself. "I was taken to Ireland in captivity with so many thousand men. And there (for before this I did not know the true God), the Lord opened to me the sense of my unbelief, that though late I might remember my sins." God "pitied my youth and ignorance, and took care of me before I knew Him . . . so I cannot keep silence concerning so great benefits and so much favour as the Lord has granted me in the land of captivity." Poor lad, he was but sixteen. But when fifteen he had committed some sin which he confessed to some amiable friend who, thirty years after, used the knowledge, fortunately without avail, to try and prevent his being made a Bishop. This tells us that he was consecrated when he was about forty-five. He was probably born about A.D. 395, carried captive about A.D. 411, escaped about A.D. 417, began his mission to Ireland about A.D. 425, and was consecrated Bishop about A.D. 440, possibly earlier. These dates, which are taken by a comparison of accounts, sometimes conflicting, fit in well with William of Malmesbury's dates in the Antiquities of Glastonbury,[1] if we do not accept the date of birth as early as A.D. 361, but accept the year A.D. 472 as that of his death. This would make him 77, instead of 111, at his death, a very old man for those days.

William says that St. Patrick was sent to Ireland in A.D. 425, and that Ireland was converted in A.D. 433. Probus, who gives us one copy of the "Confessions," says that St. Patrick began his mission as a Priest. William of Malmesbury tells us that St. Germanus, after his Alleluia Victory over the heathen Angles, ere he returned from Britain took St. Patrick into his company, "and sent him some years afterwards by the command of Pope Celestine to preach to the Irish." He also tells us that he finally returned to Britain, and lived a blameless life at Glastonbury, and "he rested in the old Church, at the right side of the Altar, for many years, for 710 years, namely, up to the time the said Church was burnt, when his body was gathered into a pyramid of stones beside the Altar, towards the South, which out of veneration for this Saint was afterwards nobly clothed in gold and silver by the diligence of his housemates."[2] Seven hundred and ten years carries us to 1182, nearly the date of the fire in A.D. 1184. His death

[1] Cap. 10.
[2] Cap. 10.

may have been in 474 or round figures may have been used. This about the fire is an interpolation after William's day.

But previous to his death St. Patrick was to organise and further develop the Celtic settlement living in huts near the Chalice Well, started by St. Fagan and St. Dyfan, in imitation of and succession to St. Joseph's first missionaries. "And Patrick, after having faithfully obeyed orders there" (in Ireland) "coming to Britain to end his days, rejecting his former dignity and salutations in the market place, landed in Cornwall at his own Altar,[1] which till this day is regarded by the inhabitants with great veneration, both for its sanctity and usefulness as well as its power to heal the sick. Coming thence to Glastonbury, and finding these twelve brethren living as hermits, he gathered them together, and accepted the office of Abbot, teaching them a community life."

Besides tradition, and written historical statement, there is circumstantial evidence that St. Patrick of Ireland ended his days and was buried in Glaston. William of Malmesbury saw the Irish constantly visiting his shrine. "Hence it became a fixed habit with the Irish to visit the place to kiss their patron's relics," he says.[2] We know that the Irish poured over here viâ Bristol from Wexford in the middle ages. We know that about three-quarters of a mile out of Glastonbury is Beckery, once an island consigned to Irish settlers. Beckery, which is also the name of an island in Wexford Harbour, is said to be a corruption of Beg Eri, meaning Little Ireland, and on the big Ordnance map both names, Beckery and Little Ireland, still appear.[3] We know, too, that there was a settlement of Irish monks here as late as St. Dunstan's day, he being taught as a boy at Glastonbury by them. Further, St. Benignus, or St. Beonna, St. Patrick's successor in Ireland, is recorded to have been also his successor here.[4] And St. Bride undoubtedly came here, and settled for a time. We are told that St. David of Wales gave the great Sapphire Altar[5] to Glastonbury partly "because of the venerable antiquity of the spot, and specially because the relics of St. Patrick and other Saints were treasured there, as may plainly be read and proved in his Acts."[6] There is an ancient Chapel of St. Patrick still standing in the old Abbey grounds.[7]

---

[1] Padstow—Patrick's Stow.
[2] C. 12, and his History of the Kings, Bk. I, C. 2.
[3] V. later. under St. Bride, p. 19.
[4] V. later, under St. Benignus, pp. 18-19.
[5] V. later, under St. David, pp. 27-28.
[6] De Antiquitate, C. 30.
[7] V. later page 44 and the Author's "St. Joseph of Arimathea at Glastonbury."

It used to be pleaded constantly by sceptics that nothing was ever heard of St. Patrick at Glastonbury before William of Malmesbury wrote. And people of the mental type that think all ancient historians rogues, unlearned, or fools, decided that the monks of his time and he were responsible for hatching the story. If we had had wide and unbroken series of histories, and an unbroken silence on the point for nearly 700 years, there would have been a prima facie case for such a charge. But the histories written were few, and those that remain are fewer. Now, however, even the silence has been broken. The discovery of the Bosworth Psalter has carried back the story that St. Patrick the Apostle of Ireland lies at Glastonbury, about 150 years earlier than William of Malmesbury, to the time of St. Dunstan. In the absence of records the critics ramp. They have a free field, and it is like cultivating microbes in a congenial soil. One is grateful for every crumb of discovery that limits their imagination or want of it. The present Dean of Wells tells us that this Psalter " was almost certainly written for St. Dunstan's use at Canterbury . . . St. Benedict's division of the Psalter is marked throughout, showing that the book was written for a monastic, and not for a secular Church . . . and its worn corners testify to a diligent use in choir. To this remarkable book a calendar is prefixed in two folios of a somewhat finer vellum written later, but as it would seem, at no great distance of date." (He shews that it is between A.D. 988 and 1023.) " A comparison of this calendar with that of the Leofric Missal proves that both are derived from a Calendar of St. Dunstan's own Abbey of Glastonbury, but the writer of the Bosworth copy has adapted it by some additions and omissions to the needs of Canterbury. . . The Calendar of Glastonbury, now that we can reconstruct it for the great days of St. Dunstan's rule, has a quite exceptional interest. . . . Let us note then some of the Saints of the British Isles, who are named in this old Glastonbury calendar. First the Irish Saints :—

> " ST. PATRICK, *Senior in Glaston.*
> " ST. PATRICK, *Bishop.*
> " ST. BRIDGET.

" St. Patrick does not surprise us : for we know that in Dunstan's boyhood Irish pilgrims came to visit his tomb—though some men said that it was not his, but the tomb of a later namesake. Our calendar allows for both." [1] So that on the whole we may safely say on the grounds

[1] Dean Armitage Robinson's " The Times of St. Dunstan," pp. 98-100.

of ancient history, ancient tradition, and the pilgrimages and veneration of the Irish, that there is more evidence for saying that St. Patrick, the Apostle of the Irish, died and was buried at Glastonbury in A.D. 472 than at any other place. If we accept this, William's story of his great work here becomes entrancing. St. Patrick "found certain brethren imbued with the rudiments of the Catholic faith, and of godly life, who had succeeded the disciples of Saints Phagan and Deruvian ; he names them, says they were of noble birth, ' desiring to adorn their nobility with works of faith,' and so had chosen a hermit life, and as he found them humble and quiet, so he preferred to be cast away with them rather than to live in royal courts. As they were all of one heart and one soul, they decided to live, eat, and drink together, and sleep in the same house. He says they placed him at their head, unwilling though he was, for he felt that he was not worthy even to unloose the latchets of their shoes. They thus led a monastic life together according to the probable pattern of the fathers. . . . Many years later, along with his brethren of Wells, he penetrated through the thick woods, and with great difficulty climbed to the top of the mountain in that island " (the Tor), " where they found an old oratory almost in ruins " (St. Michael's), " yet fitted for Christian worship, and as it seemed to him chosen by God. When they had entered they were filled with a sweet odour such as we believe to be found in the pleasant fields of Paradise. On examining the place intently they discovered a single volume in which was written the Acts of the Apostles and the Acts and Deeds of Saints Phagan and Deruvian, the greater part of it destroyed, but at the end of the volume was a document which said that the Saints Phagan and Deruvian had built the said oratory by revelation of the Lord Jesus Christ, in honour of St. Michael the Archangel, in order that he might be there perpetually honoured by men by command of God. . . . That these things are true we have proved from the testimony of the most ancient writings, and from the traditions of the elders. This Saint then, who was the Apostle of the Irish, and the first Abbot in the Isle of Avallonia " (Glastonbury), " after he had suitably instructed the aforesaid brethren in the disciplinary rules, and had adequately enriched the same spot with lands and posses- sions given by kings and other princes, yielded to Nature after some years, and earned burial in the Old Church on the right of the Altar an angel pointing out the spot where he was to lie, a huge flame bursting out from the same place in the sight of all who were present." [1]

[1] Cap. ix.

ST. BENIGNUS.

We are indebted to William of Malmesbury for telling us that St. Beonna or Benignus, a disciple of St. Patrick, and his third successor in his Irish Bishopric, became his immediate successor as Abbot of Glastonbury. He came there on a journey, and under a vow, in A.D. 460. There he decided, like his old master, to abandon his Irish bishopric, and to settle there. This he did. His prayers are said to have been answered by copious supplies of water, and his staff, like St. Joseph's, to have grown into a huge tree. There still remains an ancient Church of St. Benignus, now wrongly called St. Benedict's, described all down the centuries as a "Chapel dependent on St. John in Glaston," till the year 1846, when together with the Church of West Pennard it was cut off from the old Parish Church, and became a Parish Church. The Chapel is first heard of in the twelfth century, in the early part of which century the first actual existing reference to the Parish Church of Glastonbury, St. John the Baptist's, occurs, when a large portion of its tithe as the Parish Church of the Twelve Hides, together with that of East Pennard outside the Twelve Hides, was set apart for the Abbey. Neither of the Churches is named in Domesday, nor is that of St. Michael, which is known to have existed, probably because the Abbot owned all or nearly all the property. But some sixty years later St. John's is spoken of as an established Parish Church. There can be little doubt that St. John's existed at Domesday, and possibly St. Benignus too. But more likely the latter was first built shortly after the translation of the Saint's body, when the cult of the Saint received a fillip. St. Benignus was buried at Ferramere, or Fernigemere, now Mere, some three miles from Glastonbury, where the Abbots had one of their several manor houses, and a fish house, both still remaining. St. Benignus' tomb at Mere had these words on it, quoted by William :—

" In this tomb Father Beonna's bones are placed,
" Who was father of the monks here in ancient times.
" He was, in all probability, Patrick's servant for a
    long time.
" So say the Hibernians, and they call him ' Beonna.' "

An early epitaph, evidently not contemporary, showing careful acceptance of traditions, and an interesting casual allusion to the Irish connection with Glastonbury. In A.D.

901 Benignus' body was translated with honour to Glaston-bury. In 1027 the Danish King Hardicanute, in the Abbacy of Egelward or Ailward, gave a shrine in which, in the time of Abbot Thurston or Turstin, A.D. 1100-1116, some six hundred years after the Saint's death, was laid the body of St. Benignus.

ST. INDRACT.

St. Indract was another fifth century Irish Saint whom William of Malmesbury commemorates at Glastonbury. He tells us that the tradition of his coming was a great favourite. He refers to having written about him else-where. He has done so in the Acts of the Kings of England. The story is that St. Indract, with seven companions, was on his way back from a pilgrimage to Rome, and turned aside to visit St. Patrick's tomb at the " Second Rome," as Glastonbury was called because of the number of Saints buried there. They had filled their scrips with parsley— a most intimate touch—and other seeds for Ireland. Their staves were tipped with brass. Unfortunately, the natives mistook this for gold. They were all murdered in the neighbourhood of Shapwick, near Glastonbury. Some three centuries later, in the time of King Ina of the West Saxons, all their bodies were translated to Glastonbury, and buried in the Abbey Church, the Saint under a pyramidal stone on the left of the altar, the others at various spots under the pavement in the Church.[1]

ST. BRIDE.

Greatest of all the Irish Saints who had much to do with Glastonbury excepting St. Patrick was St. Bride, and along with his her memory has lingered more freshly than any other, and is fragrant still. William of Malmesbury is again our chief authority. St. Bride, or St. Bridget, came here in A.D. 488, very shortly after St. Patrick's death. She stayed at the Isle of Beckery, or Little Ireland,[2] about a mile out of Glastonbury within the Twelve Hides. It is thought that she may have established a nunnery on Weary-all Hill, where St. Joseph landed, at the foot of which is Beckery. She remained here some time, and then passed on, and finally returned to Ireland. She was doubt-less attracted by her love of St. Patrick, and found her countryman St. Benignus ruling.

At Beckery there was an oratory dedicated to St. Mary

[1] William of Malmesbury's " De Antiquitate," Cap. 12 and 20, and his " Gesta Regum," By. I, Cap. 2.
[2] V. p. 15.

Magdalen, which she probably built, hence the name of
Magdalen Street in Glastonbury, from which leads the road
to Beckery. After her departure, for some cause or
another, this gave place to a larger chapel dedicated to
St. Bride herself. And on Chamberlain Hill in Beckery,
or Northover as it is also called, is a piece of land still
called and marked in the Ordnance map as "Bride's."
Some forty years back the Somerset Archæological
Society dug at Bride's and found the remains of two very
ancient chapels, one larger than the other, and of a third
building which might have been a priest's house or St.
Bride's dwelling.

William tells us that when she left, she left behind her
(delightfully Irish !) certain articles, such as a victual bag,
a necklace, a bell, and implements for embroidery. In
William's time they " were treasured to her memory," and
they were venerated in the chapel at Beckery in John of
Glastonbury's time and until the Reformation. They then
disappeared. Quite recently St. Bride's own hand bell,
with which she rang the people to service, has almost certainly been found, and is at Chalice Well Hostel, and is the
property of Miss Alice Buckton, the authoress of "Eager
Heart," who gladly shows it to pious pilgrims. An old
Glastonbury man of slender means lost an old friend who
lived at a tiny out-of-the-way farm-house in the midst of the
moors, as the marshes are called. On his old friend's death
he wended his way thither on the day of the sale of his goods
to buy a memento. Everything was beyond his purse
except an old oak box, which he bought for five shillings,
for love of his friend, and carried back with him. When he
got home he found a roll of very old linen in it, and in that
the bell, otherwise quite perfect but minus its tongue. Alas !
the linen and the box have disappeared ! It is a woman's
bell. A man's fingers would not go through the loop at
the top, for they rang them sometimes with the hand, as
well as carried them on the top of their staff. It has been
taken to the British and Dublin Museums. Both give the
same verdict—" a most ancient Celtic bell, and there is no
reason why it should not be St. Bride's." It is very similar
to St. Patrick's at Dublin, but smaller. Metals are
annealed by a process now lost. Its sound is most true and
musical. The author recently had the pleasure of taking
Professor R. A. S. Macalister, Professor of Celtic Archæ-
ology at Dublin, to see it. He expressed the greatest
delight at the discovery, and hopes to write an account of
it.

Bride returned to Ireland and died there, and another

and later hand writes in the margin of William of Malmesbury's "*De Antiquitate Glastoniae*" : "The Patrick who died in Ireland was also born there, and was Bishop there about the year 850 A.D., and he, buried, there was translated in the reign of King Henry II, the son of the Empress Matilda, with the Saints Columkille and Bridget, as Giraldus Cambrensis testifieth in his Topographia Hiberniae, and although St. Columkille, who was also called according to some St. Columba, and St. Bridget were translated along with this Patrick, they were not contemporaries, for St. Bridget lived towards the end of the life of St. Patrick the elder, of whom we treated above. For she outlived him, so Gildas writes, sixty years, and came to Glastonia about the year of the Lord 488.[1] St. Columkille was born four years before the death of St. Bridget, and she herself came to Glastonbury a generation after, about the year 504. These two, indeed, along with not a few Irish nobles, frequented the spot out of veneration for their patron St. Patrick. . . . St. Bridget returned to Ireland, where she fell asleep in the Lord not long afterwards, and was buried in the City of Down along with Patrick and Columba together in one tomb, as appears from the tomb's epitaph :

"'Here are entombed in one tomb in Down,
"'Bridget, Patrick, and good Columba.'"

Although St. Bride only stayed a few years at Glaston, yet here, as everywhere else where she passed, she made such an impression that we find her carved milking her cow upon the superb Norman northern doorway to St. Joseph's chapel (St. Mary's) at the Abbey, and on the tower of St. Michael's Church on the Tor, built after an earthquake had destroyed the older Church there in 1275. Where she trod they carved her in stone.

Bride had a mysterious charm. Wherever she passed the world was not quite the same again. There was a new freshness in the breeze, a new brilliance in the flowers. And the mellow sound of her bell when struck still charms. In St. Patrick's chapel in the old churchyard where once they two and St. David walked, in one sublime succession, it is heard on St. Bride's Day, and seems to reconsecrate that most holy spot, and give it a sanctity that never fades from the memory. At the sound of that bell the people

[1] Nennius says " From the nativity of Our Lord to the coming of St. Patrick among the Scots " (in Ireland) " are computed 405 years " (20 less than William of Malmesbury and some others compute) " from the death of St. Patrick to that of St. Bridget 40 years "—20 less than attributed to St. Gildas above—and from the birth of Columkille to the death of St. Bridget four years.

whom she summoned to worship seem to start from their sleep, and she, who never sleeps, appears to become visible with them. Mysterious little woman, the daughter of a king, the friend of the simple, who for our sakes became poor, she has indeed a most undying memory. A female St. Paul, like him she has reconsecrated an amazing part of the earth's surface. They are ever passing on their way. But they never pass out of history. They are the inspiration of the whole human race, and a whisper of what it may become. Paul the aged! Bride of the Isles! So bewilderingly, fascinatingly elusive! So tangibly, abidingly real!

It is interesting to note that when William of Malmesbury wrote the Acts of the Kings of England, he said about St. Bride : "Whether Bridget returned home or died at Glastonbury is not sufficiently ascertained." [1] But when he had stayed at the Abbey, surveyed everything, read everything, heard everything, and weighed everything on the subject, he was quite conclusive on that point. "St. Bridget, indeed, who came here A.D. 488, after a short stay in an island called Beckery, returned home." [2] And a marginal note by a later hand already quoted says : " She returned to Ireland, where she fell asleep in the Lord not long afterwards." [3] This disposes of the suggestion that the monks were unscrupulous gasconaders, and William credulous. Dean Armitage Robinson has shown that the Calendar attached to the Bosworth Psalter proves that St. Bride's connection with Glastonbury was current tradition there in St. Dunstan's time in the tenth century. [4]

ST. COLUMBA.

St. Columba, like St. Bride, was of royal Irish lineage, and in his case on both sides, and was related to Conel, King of the Scots, in North Britain, though he himself was born in Ireland—probably at Gartom, in Donegal.

William of Malmesbury is quite definite that the feet of St. Columba trod the holy Churchyard of Glastonbury. And doubtless he is right. It was only natural that he should follow in the steps of St. Benignus and St. Bride, and visit the grave of St. Patrick. And this was not the only incentive. William writes : " The Church, of which

---

[1] Acts of the Kings, Bk. I, Cap. 2.
[2] De Antiquitate, Cap. 12.
[3] De Antiquitate, Cap. 2.
[4] V. pp. 16 and Dean Robinson's " Times of St. Dunstan," pp. 100-1.

we write, frequently called 'the Old Church' by the Angles because of its antiquity, built first of rushes, *from the very beginning* breathed out and spread abroad throughout the entire country a mysterious odour of Divine sanctity, from the cult of a great devotion, rude though it may have been. *Hence the confluence hither of all kinds of people along all the paths of the sea; hence the great show of rich treasures deposited here; hence the constant succession of religious and literary men."* He tells us : " A.D. 504 St. Columba came to Glaston. Some affirm that this Saint finished his course there, but whether he did or whether he returned to his own country, I will not asseverate." In the marginal note to Cap. 2 by a later hand already referred to[2] under St. Bridget, he is called Columkille, and spoken of as a female. We read : " St. Columkille was born four years before the death of St. Bridget, and she herself came to Glastonbury a generation afterwards, about the year 504. These two, indeed, along with not a few Irish nobles, frequented the spot out of veneration for their patron, St. Patrick." The date 504 is difficult to fit in with our present knowledge. St. Columba is said to have been born December 7th, 521. What stands out is that William and his annotator both believed in his having come here, and that cautious William, after hearing and seeing the best evidence that he could get on the spot, could not decide whether he died here or returned. We may therefore feel practically certain that it was only a temporary sojourn here.

We can safely accept the beautiful story of St. Columba's death in Iona on June 9th, 597. For within sixty years of his death his successor, Abbot Cuminius, wrote his life, only to be followed by Abbot Adamnan in less than a quarter of a century. His own Iona was full of his story and his influence, and these two wrote out of their intimate knowledge. Every nook spoke of him, and Venerable Bede adds touches to the picture. We tread on safe ground when we, having read what William of Malmesbury could not read, accept and tell the charming story of St. Columba's death. Knowing that his end was near on Saturday, June 8th, with the aid of a favourite monk he climbed the little hill overlooking his beloved monastery, and fondly gave his parting blessing to the spot that meant so much to him, at once the centre and crown of his life's work. Looking round with loving eyes he left that summer scene, and returned to his cell to continue a transcription of the Psalms. The last words

[1] De Antiquitate, C. 6. He was an eye-witness.
[2] V. p. 21.

which he wrote were : " They who seek the Lord shall
want no manner of thing that is good," in the 34th Psalm.
He then said : " Here I must stop ; what follows let
Baithen write." The words that follow are : " Come, ye
children, and hearken unto me, and I will teach you the
fear of the Lord." So it was considered that he had
pointed to Baithen as his successor as Abbot. That
evening he was present in the little Abbey Church, and
again at midnight. But it was too much for him. He
sank down before the altar, and his soul returned to God
who gave it.

But doubtless, though he died in Iona, his feet trod
the sacred soil of Avalon. How amazingly these British
saints travelled on foot through almost trackless lands and
through the deep in cockle shells ! God took their passion
for voyaging, their adventurous restlessness, and consecrated it to Himself. And so Columba links Iona and
Glastonbury with all that they stand for in Celtic church
history. St. Columbanus, too, also an Irish monk, born
in the next generation, about A.D. 550, and brought up
at the ancient British monastery of Bangor, seems to link
Glastonbury with the monasteries which he founded at
Luxeuil in the Vosges, and Bobbio in Italy. His method
of keeping Easter, and his fearless denunciation of the
crimes of Thierry II. of Burgundy, and of the Queen-
mother, Brune-haut, his refusal to retract, and even to
depart except under *force majeure,* were typically British.
He was expelled from Burgundy in company with St. Gall,
also brought up with him at Bangor Monastery, thus
linking the British Celtic Church with St. Gall in Switzerland. St. Columbanus' knowledge of Latin, Greek and
Hebrew were astonishing. Study may have brought him
to Glastonbury. There was a chapel dedicated to him in
the Forest of Cheddar, hard by Glastonbury, and another
at Culbane, near Porlock, in Somerset, an evident corruption of his name, which also possibly survives in Cullomp-
ton in Devon ; so that, Glastonbury being what it was to
Britain, we may pretty confidently believe that St. Columba
came here and that St. Columbanus, his compatriot and
almost contemporary, made it his headquarters at some
period of his work.

ST. DAVID OF WALES.

Perhaps no one ever loved Glastonbury quite so much
as St. David of Wales. William tells us : " How highly
this spot was esteemed in those days this great man, David,

Archbishop of St. David's, has testified more than need
be illustrated by our relation." The Reverend Rice Rees[1]
says that he was of royal descent, the son of the Prince
of Cardigan, and was born at Menevia. The date of his
birth is unknown. He is said to have died at the age of
82, but the date of his death varies from about A.D. 542
(Geoffrey of Monmouth), A.D. 544 (Archbishop Ussher),
A.D. 546 (William of Malmesbury), to A.D. 601 (Annales
Cambriae). Haddan and Stubbs accept the latter.[2] He
was brought up at the college of Paulinus, a great teacher.
He founded a monastery with a school in the Rhos Valley
near Menevia, which was a very strict rule. He took a
very leading part at the Synod of Brefi in confuting the
Pelagian heresy. The Synod elected him Archbishop of
Caerleon on Usk, one of the three great Celtic archbishoprics, the others being London and York. He finally
removed the seat of his Archbishopric to his birthplace,
Menevia, which afterwards became St. David's. His
earliest historian was Ricemarchus, Bishop of St. David's
in the 11th century. But William of Malmesbury has much
to tell us about him in the 12th, and especially his great
passion for Glastonbury.

William deals especially with three things :—

1. St. David's building and dedication of a Church at
   Glastonbury ;

2. St. David's gift of the Sapphire Altar ;

3. Where does St. David lie ?

Let us take each of these in turn.

1. "He learnt of the antiquity and sanctity of the
("Olde") Church by a Divine oracle. Being therefore bent
on dedicating it, he came to the spot accompanied by seven
bishops of whom he was Primate." One wonders whether he
intended to dedicate it to St. Patrick, whom he very greatly
venerated. Old dedications were not infrequently changed
of yore. William tells us this tale. The night before the
dedication service the Saint went to sleep, and saw Our
Lord standing by his bed. Asking in gentle tones why
they had come, and learning why, the Saviour replied that
"The Church had been dedicated long ago by Himself in
honour of His Mother, and it was not seemly that it should
be re-dedicated by human hands." Our Lord then touched
the palm of his hand with His finger, which made a hole in
it, and added, "Let him take that for a sign that he might

[1] Welsh Saints.
[2] Councils and Ecclesiastical Documents.

not repeat what Himself had done beforehand. But, because
his intention had not been so much a bold as a devout one,
his punishment should not be prolonged. Finally, on the
following morning, when he was going to say the words in
the Mass, 'through Him, and with Him, and in Him,' the
full strength of salvation should flow back to him.'' The
Primate awoke. It is not quite clear whether William only
considered it a vision, or one that was actually fulfilled.
It rather appears that he thought the latter. The narrative
ends up : ''But lest they should seem to have come out for
nought, he set about building and dedicating another
Church.' This is very interesting, for later on William
gives an ''Excursus on the four Churches of Glastonbury.'' '
They are as follows :—

> 1st and oldest.—St. Joseph's, West of all the others.
>
> 2nd.—St. David's, East of the old Church, in honour
> of St. Mary, when forbidden to dedicate the Old
> Church.
>
> 3rd.—One built by twelve men from the North of
> Britain, also East of the Old Church.
>
> 4th and largest.—King Ina's, in honour of Our Lord
> and Saints Peter and Paul, East of all the rest,
> for the sake of the soul of his brother Mules, whom
> the Kentish people burnt below Canterbury.

This takes no account of the Oratory built by Saints Fagan
and Deruvian on to the Old Church, which they dedicated
to Saints Peter and Paul.' That St. David's was the first
to the East is supported by a very ancient inscription.

Sammes' Antiquities of Ancient Britain⁴ gives an
inscription on a brass plate fastened to a pillar in the great
Abbey Church of Glastonbury, which remained there till
the Dissolution,⁵ and was to be seen in Wells, in the
possession of a Mr. Hughes, of Wells, as late as 1639.
This confirms the claim that St. David was the first
person to build on to the Old Church. It tells of
its foundation by St. Joseph and his eleven companions,
of St. David's frustrated intention to dedicate it, and of
his adding instead a sort of chancel '' quendam cancellum.''
It goes on expressly to say : '' And lest the site or size of

---

¹ De Antiquitate, C. 15.
² De Antiquitate, C. 39.
³ De Antiquitate, C. 2.
⁴ p. 212.
⁵ Warner's '' History of the Abbey of Glastonbury,'' Appendix pp.
9 and 39.

the Church should be forgotten through such additions,"
St. David erected a pillar to the North of the East end of the
Church. The distance of the centre of this pillar from the
centre of the East end of the Church, and the length and
breadth of the Church are given. This, of course, was the
Old Wattle Church. The present Norman one was not
built till after the Fire in A.D. 1184. St. David's determination to preserve the sanctity and identity of the Old Church
is most valuable. Suffice it to say that in July, 1921,
inspired by this inscription, Dean Robinson of Wells
ordered the foundations of this column to be dug for,
measuring from the centre of the Norman Church, and the
position of this 1400 years old column exactly tallied with
this inscription, as did the size of the Norman Church,
shewing that the Henry II. builders had exactly the same
intention of preserving the site and size of the old Church
as St. David, and carried it out. It is an unique care of
an unique site.

2. Besides building on to the Old Church "because
of the increase in the number of Saints in the same," [1] St.
David gave Glastonbury one of its most celebrated treasures,
the great Sapphire Altar. William tells how one night in
his Monastery in the Ross Valley an angel bade St. David
go to Jerusalem next day with two of his household. The
Saint obeyed. The gift of tongues was given to him. The
night before their arrival at Jerusalem an angel told the
Patriarch of Jerusalem of their coming arrival, and bade him
welcome them. The Patriarch rejoiced, and on their
arrival invoked their aid against the Jews, who were wax-
ing stronger and more aggressive every day. They
preached so vehemently and successfully that the hands of
the Christians were greatly strengthened, and many
unbelievers were converted. On their departure for Britain
the Patriarch gave St. David a consecrated Altar, a wonderful bell, a staff, and a tunic woven with gold. These were
sent after them. "But," says William, of the Altar, "St.
David, desiring that such a treasure should have a worthy
custodian when he had gone, bequeathed the stone to the
Church of Glastonbury while he was yet alive, which Church
he embraced with a wonderful affection because of the
venerable antiquity of the spot, and specially because the
relics of St. Patrick and other Saints were treasured there,
as may be plainly read and proved in his Acts. The said
Altar is therefore exhibited to this day in the Church of
Glastonbury in memory of the said Saint, not preserved by
human effort, but by Divine Providence, who amid the con-

[1] From the above-named inscription.

stant whirl of change, and the succession of kings and king-
doms, amid the heaviest storms of warfare, when all else
had been overturned or removed, continued to keep the
greedy hands of foes aloof from this treasure." [1] He goes
on to tell how this Altar had been hidden in time of war,
and long lost, and then found by Henry of Blois, brother of
King Stephen, Bishop of Winchester and Abbot of Glastonbury, in a doorway in St. Mary's Church, and how he
had " adorned it magnificently with gold and silver, and
precious stones, as it is now." In Frank Lomax's
translation of William's Antiquity of Glastonbury,[2] it is
suggested that in two half plaques of Limoges enamel at
the British Museum depicting Henry of Blois holding a
portable Altar, and inscribed with fulsome praise of him,
we have a portrayal of the Sapphire Altar of Glastonbury.
It is quite likely. No one knows what became of the great
sapphire from which it takes its name. When the Cardinal
of York, grandson of the Elder Pretender, was dying in
Italy, a most astounding thing happened. He sent to
George III. of England a great sapphire. Some think this
was the Glastonbury sapphire, stolen by Henry VIII. If
so, it may yet be in the Crown Jewels, if it escaped some
of George IV.'s ladies. An imperfect MS. still preserved
(given in the Appendix to Mon. Ang. No. 1) of an inventory
of the spoils of the Monasteries, says : " Item : delyvered
more unto his Majestie the same day " (25th May in the
31st year of his reign) " of the same stuffe, a superaltare,
garnished with silver and gilte, called the greate saphire
of Glassonburye." [3] This inventory not only traces this
Altar to the Crown, but by the description super-altar shows
that it was a portable Altar, or travelling Altar, such as
was used by missionaries, in war time, and in private
chapels by the Bishop's licence. This fits the story of its
origin. The earliest existing portable Altar was found
on the breast of St. Cuthbert, who died A.D. 687, when his
coffin was opened in 1827. It is oak covered with silver,
some of which is lost, and is six inches long and five and a
quarter inches broad. It has an inscription in honour of
St. Peter.[4] Pilgrims used to come on purpose to see and
venerate the Sapphire Altar. This story of St. David
going to Jerusalem in the 6th century is quite in keeping
with what St. Jerome tells us in his Epistle to Marcella
in the 4th. " The Britons, who live apart from our world,

---

[1] Cap. 30.
[2] p. 57.
[3] Warner's " History of Glastonbury," p. 156.
[4] Chas. Wall's (F.R.Hist.S.) " Short History of the Altar," pp.
14 and 15.

if they go on a pilgrimage, will leave the Western parts, and seek Jerusalem, known to them by fame only, and by the Scriptures.''[1] The trend of evidence seems to shew that the early Celtic Church looked to Jerusalem and not to Rome as their Patriarchate. It was Eastern in origin. It is quite significant that out of 318 Bishops at the Council of Arles in A.D. 314, at which three British Bishops were present, hardly ten were of the Latin-speaking Church. Celtic saints of the same generation as St. Augustine of Canterbury were planting monasteries on the Continent, although large tracts of their own country were over-run by the hated Saxon, who would never have listened to them. Thus St. Columbanus, born about 550, founded Luxeuil in Burgundy, and Bobbio in Italy, while his fellow student at Bangor and fellow missionary in Burgundy, St. Gall, founded St. Gall in Switzerland.[2] Glastonbury itself was only brought under Rome, according to 12th century admissions, as an isolated act by King Ina between A.D. 725 and 728.[3] This story of the pilgrimage of St. David to Jerusalem is only in keeping with other evidence as to the attitude of respectful reverence to the Church of Jerusalem rather than to Rome on the part of the independent Celtic Church. The frequency of chapels in churches dedicated to saints connected with the East, like St. Catherine, St. Margaret, St. Nicholas and St. George (with his Eastern adventures), all point in the same direction.

3. Where does St. David lie? He was undoubtedly buried at Menevia, or St. David's, in his Cathedral Church. But did he remain there? After recording that he died in A.D. 546, William says : " Some indeed say that the remains of this holy and incomparable man were mingled with those of St. Patrick in the Old Church, and the Welsh without doubt support and corroborate this by their frequent orations, and manifold asseverations, putting this in the foreground—that Bernard, the Bishop of the Ross Valley, had there sought for the relics of the dead Saint once and again, and, many denying it, had not found them. But we will subjoin an account of how the said relics were translated from the Ross Valley to Glastonbury. ' A certain dame, named Aelswitha, in the reign of King Edgar, acquired the said relics through a relative of hers, who at that time was Bishop over the Ross Valley, when all that district was so devastated that scarce one mortal could be

[1] See Hadan and Stubbs, I., 10.
[2] V. pp. 7 and 12.
[3] V. p. 47.

found in it—only a few women, and these in few places—
and she placed the relics at Glastonbury. Certain
Welshmen from yonder religious land testify that they,
journeying to Rome in those days, brought with them to
Glastonbury very many bodies of Saints and reliques, and
proceeding on their journey, left them there. This translation was made in the 420th year after the death of the
same, A.D. 962.' " This date is rather interesting, as it
makes the year of the death the same as Geoffrey of Monmouth's, A.D. 542. It looks as if William had heard and
accepted this date, but after careful inquiry had decided on
546, and had forgotten to alter the original computation of
the date of the translation, or, if he were certain of the
latter, had forgotten to re-adjust his arithmetical sum.

There is the story. Certain it is that Glastonbury all
down the ages was marvellously preserved from pillage
till a traitor within the fold in the person of Henry VIII.
accomplished it. The Romans never got full grip of this
part of the kingdom, the Saxons never got here till they
were Christians, and when at last the Danes arrived,
Canute covered King Edmund's tomb in the Abbey Church
with a pall woven apparently of peacocks' feathers,[1] and
Hardicanute gave a shrine, ultimately the resting-place of
St. Benignus.[2] Compare this with the horrors done by
heathen Saxon to Christian Celt, and heathen Dane to
Christian Saxon in other parts of the kingdom. Ravaged
Churches and Monasteries sent their blessed dead and their
treasures and their sons to what was at once the Bethlehem
and Jerusalem of Britain for protection. Truly it was
guarded by the Eye and Hand of God. And we must come
to the conclusion, while gratefully acknowledging the work
of the monks here and elsewhere, so needed in their age,
that had this great Abbey remained true to God and herself,
had there been less quarrelling, less greed, less haughtiness
—(it is a very unedifying story)—and more simple religion,
He would have guarded it to this day. St. Dunstan, the
last of the great Saints, was the first of the great politicians.
The two things do not blend. The latter was the death-
knell of the former. St. Dunstan did not wish to lead the
religious life. His uncle forced him. It was probably very
good for St. Dunstan, he being a supreme genius, able to
unite success in this and success in many other callings.
It was probably very bad ultimately for the Church, as others
tried to unite the rôles, and most of them failed.

[1] De Antiquitate, Cap. 58.
[2] V. p. 19.

KING ARTHUR.

I here venture to insert a Saint never canonized, a Saint whose spell was so great, and deeds so glorious, that he has suffered more than most men from his chroniclers, and from the love of the unlearned, which wove fables like mists around a treasured memory. Not last but perhaps greatest romantic leader of a romantic people in a dying cause, he has been beatified and enshrined in legend by common consent. And the prosaic, and—(shall I say?)—automata fail to discern him. But as John S. Stuart-Glennie says of him : " Behind these " (myths and legends) " is the original Arthur." . . . " There was a real Arthur, one of the last Celtic chiefs in Great Britain." [1] But, alas, on the subject of King Arthur, the Dean of Wells with his blend of active imagination and cool criticism, somewhat suddenly fails us. We are eternally grateful to him for the words which he penned on St. Patrick : " The abbots of Glastonbury, therefore, though some of their names can no longer be traced, go back to the first half of the fifth century. St. Patrick was the first, and St. Benignus, his pupil, was the second. We may question this to-day, if we will, as Ralph Higden questioned it in the fourteenth century, and suppose that there has been some confusion with a later Patrick. But if we had lived in William of Malmesbury's time, and seen St. Patrick's tomb with the Irish pilgrims kneeling round it, and had copied the epitaph of St. Benignus at Mere, and visited St. Bridget's Chapel at Beckery, or Little Ireland, and seen her wallet and her distaff, we should have been sceptical indeed had we accused the historian of excessive credulity." [2]

Yet the Dean rejects the story in William of Malmesbury's De Antiquitate of the discovery of the body of King Arthur at Glastonbury. He does so on the ground that William of Malmesbury in his earlier book, The Acts of the Kings of England, [3] when telling of the discovery in Wales in A.D. 1087 of the grave of Walwin, Arthur's nephew, adds : " The sepulchre of Arthur is nowhere to be seen whence ancient ballads fable that he is still to come." The Acts of the Kings was written about 1125 and later editions were edited in 1138 and 1140. The De Antiquitate was written between 1129 and 1139. If William had been convinced of the truth of the burial of Arthur at Avalon between writing the latter and re-editing the former, he might very

[1] King Arthur, Encycl. Brit. (8th Edn.), Vol. II., p. 649.
[2] Somerset Historical Essays. William of Malmesbury on " The Antiquity of Glastonbury," pp. 23-4.
[3] Book III., p. 315, Bohn's edition.

well have overlooked the correction of a mere obiter dictum, if he ever did re-edit his book himself. And the latest date for the De Antiquitate, and the latest date for the last edition of the Acts are so close, that one can imagine many reasons accounting for the non-correction in such a case. One hopes that the spell of Glastonbury, still further kindling the Dean's sympathy, and closer investigation stimulating a rather timid criticism, may yet lead to some grateful verdict to live in our hearts and memories.

Meantime, let us humbly tell the story. As has before been pointed out, it is very dangerous to accentuate the silences in ancient history. For instance, Bede, writing an Ecclesiastical history, never mentions the existence of St. Patrick.[1] Anyway, this fact stands out : Geoffrey of Monmouth and William of Malmesbury, two Norman monks, much about the same time tell us of King Arthur the Celt. The Normans and Saxons were certainly not inclined to aggrandize the Celts. Geoffrey writing before A.D. 1147 (if the Book of Brutus alluded to by William of Malmesbury be Geoffrey's History of the Britains, it must be well before that), comments on the silence of Gildas and Bede on King Arthur and many others, and tells how Walter, Archdeacon of Oxford, possibly Walter Mapes, had given him a very ancient Celtic MS. which he proceeds to translate. He tells how, on the death of Arthur's father, the kingdom being sore beset by the Saxons, Arthur was crowned at the age of fifteen by Dubricius, Archbishop of Caerleon, who afterwards made way for St. David. After much war, in which he was successful, bearing the Blessed Virgin and Child painted inside his shield,[2] that he might gain inspiration by looking at them, and carrying his famous sword Calliburn, which was made at Avalon (Glastonbury), he summoned a mighty assembly at Caerleon on Usk for the Feast of Pentecost, when all the mighty of the kingdom were assembled, together with the three Archbishops of London, York, and Caerleon, that the latter (still Dubricius) might crown him again with great pomp in time of peace. Then follows an account of Arthur's foreign wars, and how when he was on the verge of striking a blow at Rome itself, he was recalled by the news that Guinevere had run away with his nephew Modred, and that Modred had set up the standard of revolt. Arthur landed at Richborough in Kent,

---

[1] And he refers to the absence of snakes in Ireland ! !

[2] The Arms of Glastonbury are the Arms ascribed by the Heralds to Arthur, a cross, with the Virgin and Child in the first quarter of the shield, because of the Vision of the Blessed Virgin and Child that he is said to have had on Weary-All Hill, Glastonbury, where St. Joseph landed.

fought a great battle there which made great havoc of both armies. Modred fled to Winchester. There he was again defeated, after a terrible battle, and fled to Cornwall. Arthur followed. Near the River Camba a furious battle was fought, where Modred and the flower of both armies were killed. We read : " And even the renowned King Arthur himself was mortally wounded, and being carried thence to the Isle of Avalon " (Glastonbury) " to be cured of his wounds, he gave up the crown of his kingdom to his kinsman Constantine, the son of Cador, Duke of Cornwall, in the 542nd year of Our Lord's Incarnation," in the same year, it will be noted, as is ascribed to the death of St. David, who is sometimes spoken of as the uncle of King Arthur.

Before this Norman writer, the earliest authors who refer to this celebrated king and his conquests, are his own countrymen, Llwyarch, a bard and king, born about A.D. 480, the bard and prophet Myrdhinn, afterwards called Merlin, who was Arthur's teacher, Taliessin, and Aneurin. It is interesting that Geoffrey of Monmouth's first work was a translation in Latin of the Prophecies of Merlin, which he wrote at the request of Alexander, Bishop of Lincoln. Geoffrey of Monmouth and William of Malmesbury both dedicated some of their literary work to Robert of Gloucester, natural son of Henry I. Is it not, therefore, reasonable to suppose that they may have known or corresponded with each other ? And is it not natural to think that these two Norman monks had some source of information which we have not got ? Glastonbury Abbey Library was one of the finest in the world. William constantly refers to " ancient writings," " a history of Britain," and " Writings of the ancients." Leland, going to Glastonbury Abbey shortly before its dissolution, was amazed at its marvellous library, and specifically mentions a Celtic sixth century history, or rather a portion of one, written by Melchin of Avalon. And Archbishop Ussher, also as late as the sixteenth century, refers to an old Welsh History in the Cottonian Library which, he says, some thought to be the very one which Geoffrey copied.[1]

Let us turn to the account of the other Norman. Let us see then what William tells, and how it tallies with Geoffrey's account. He tells us how Arthur gave to Brent Knoll and Poldone chalices and other ornaments for eighty monks to pray for the soul of his friend Ider the son of King Nuth.[2] In the margin of Cap. 2 a very old hand-writing, but not the same hand as in the text,[3] makes a

[1] De. Brit. Eccl. Prim., Cap. 5.
[2] C. 34.
[3] V. Lomax' translation of De Antiquitate, p. 135.

reference to Lancelot of the lake, King Arthur, and the Holy Grail, and to " the Book of the Acts of the illustrious King Arthur." [1]   In Cap. xxxi. we are told that " Arthur the illustrious King of the Britons," was " buried in the Monks Cemetery between two pyramidal stones along with his spouse."   That " in the year of the Lord's incarnation 542 he was mortally wounded by Modredus in Cornwall, close by the River Camba, and proceeded thence to the Isle of Avallonia to be healed of his wound, where he died about Whitsuntide—the date is a realistic touch.   And in the margin, in what Mr. Lomax says is " handwriting of like antiquity, although a little different and in paler ink " we read : "After the war at Kemeler in Cornwall, where Modred was killed . . . when this same Arthur himself was mortally wounded, his body was born to Isle of Avallonia (now called Glastonbury) by a certain noble dame, a relative of his called Morganis ; and when he afterwards died he was buried in the same sacred cemetery by her means.   That is why the romance-weaving Britons and their bards used to tell how an imaginary goddess named Morganis bore the body of Arthur to the Isle of Avallonia to heal his wound ; and after this is healed the King will return, strong and powerful, to rule the Britons (so they say) as of yore, in consequence of which they look for his return to this day, as the Jews still expect their Messiah, for our ancestors were deceived by foolishness and incongruity as well as by infidelity."   Here we have both monks giving the same account of his death, and both saying that he was carried to Avalon to be healed of his wounds, and William goes further. He tells us the place of his burial along with poor Guinevere in the Monks' Cemetery between two pyramidal stones, the very last place where one would have expected them to be buried.   Now why was this great hero and king not buried in great pomp in the Old Church, and a great shrine made ?   Because the monks feared the desecration of his grave by the heathen Saxons.   For after him and the Celtic self-destruction which is so common to this brave race, came the deluge.   William learnt from the monks the secret of his burial place, known only to the Monastery itself.   It was no longer necessary to hide it ;

---

[1] John of Glastonbury includes this marginal note in his text. He tells us that when speaking of the quest of Sir Lancelot, "The Acts of the Illustrious King Arthur," tells us of the coming of Joseph of Arimathea, Josephes his son, and others.   He also traces King Arthur's descent through his mother from St. Joseph.   Hearne's Edition (small paper), pp. 55-7.   Apparently both the marginal note writer and John of Glastonbury are quoting from the now lost book, " The Acts of the Illustrious King Arthur."

he published it. It was one of the many testimonies that
the actual Abbey yielded to its history.

It is to be noted that William of Malmesbury actually
refers to the romances woven by the Britons round the
memory of their great King, and traces the source of one
to its foundation, and gives the true history in its place,
and shows how the devotion of a living woman became the
magic of a fabled goddess. And it is to be remembered that
it is just such a story as might be expected to be born
about Avalon. Avilion[1] was the Isle of Departed Spirits.
In Celtic days Avalon was known not only as the Royal
Isle, but as the Holy Isle. And there was a legend that
departed spirits went into the Tor, and passed out the
other side into Hades. It is curious that to this day there
is a beautiful little dell, in the primrose-time a fairy-like
place indeed, nestling at the foot of the Tor on the North
side, which is called Paradise. And I discovered in a
seventeenth century Church Terrier in the Diocesan
Registry of Wells, that there is a piece of land called Avalon
at the foot of the Tor on the other side. It may be that
that whole Isle took its name from this spot, and that in
these two ancient place-names we have a relic of the ancient
belief that it was the place of departed spirits which may
so well have brought about the legend that Arthur is not
dead, but lingers in the Isle of the Blest, thence one day
at a national crisis to return. The wish was father to the
thought. There is a somewhat similar tradition that St.
Joseph's body is to be found intact before the Day of Judg-
ment. Such traditions are unavoidable in this Isle of the
Immortals. I remember one day, some seven years ago,
little knowing that I should ever live at Glastonbury, looking from the foot of Tor Hill, Wells, at Glastonbury Tor,
bathed in sunset mists, and lights of a thousand hues. And,
as I looked, I understood all the legends that grew up
around Avalon. I repeat, they are unavoidable, but under
them is history, just as there is the real every-day Tor, and
romantic, too, behind the iridescent beauties of the mist.

But the history of Glastonbury does not stop short with
William. He was succeeded as historian by Adam de
Domerham, writing 1280—1290 A.D., who wrote of the 12th
and 13th centuries, he by John of Glastonbury, who wrote
of the 14th, he by William of Worcester, who wrote his
Itinerary between 1475 and 1480, and he by Leland, who
came and wrote just before the Reformation, and there is
also Abbot Monington's Secretum with its Charters and
Deeds of the Abbey. Writing this little account, far from
great libraries, with a love for the place and its story far

[1] Its earlier name.

greater than my time and ability to get at all the books and
MSS. which one longs to study, I have barely seen Adam
de Domerham. I am not sure what he wrote about Arthur.
I must leave this for a later time, or for others. But I have
been right through John of Glastonbury, and I know that
his story fits in with the story of the earlier Norman monks.
He tells us that Arthur died in summer about Pentecost, and
was buried there with Queen Guinevere in the Cemetery of
the Monks A.D. 542, and repeats the story of his death, and
removal to Avalon. He adds that he rested there 648
years, and afterwards, in A.D. 1190, was translated into the
greater Church.[1] He tells us later that Richard I. appointed
Henry de Soliacus (probably de Salis),[2] Prior of Bermond-
sey, a man of royal race, in 1189, the year of his coronation,
to be Abbot. He tells us that Giraldus Cambrensis says
that this Abbot was Abbot in the time of Henry II., by
whom he was frequently admonished, that he should lodge
King Arthur more decently, and move him from the depths
to a worthier status.''   Whichever king appointed him, the
admonition of Henry is of interest. (It is quite possible
that Richard merely carried out his father's intentions in
appointing Henry de Soliacus Abbot.) For the story is that
Henry II. had never heard of Arthur till a Welsh Bard came
before him and sang of him on the eve of Henry's embarka-
tion for Waterford, where he landed October 18th, 1172.
The dates fit in very well.   John of Glastonbury goes on :
" For he (Arthur) had rested next to the Old Church
between two stone pyramids, formerly nobly carved, 648
years."   The allusion to the former beauty of the carving
are the words of one who had looked on a very ancient
monument much worn. "Whence on a certain day,
surrounding the place with curtains' he" (the Abbot) "gives
the order to dig. Here, after the diggers had explored a
very great depth, when now nearly desperate, they found
a wooden coffin of enormous size, entirely closed. And
when they had lifted and opened this, they found the king's
bones of incredible size, so that the one bone of the tibia
reached from the ground to the middle of the thigh and
more in a big man.   They also found a leaden cross, having
inscribed on one side : ' Here lies buried in Avalon the
celebrated King Arthur.' From here, opening the tomb
of the Queen, they see the hair of her head lying intact
around the bones, as if she had been recently buried there,

---

[1] Hearne's (small paper) Edition, pp. 30-31.
[2] The Solly family of Kent are descended from a branch of the
de Salis family.
[3] Cortinis.

but when touched by them it completely crumbled to nothing. The Abbot therefore and convent undertaking their obsequies, translated them with joy into the greater Church into a mausoleum nobly carved, arranging it within in two parts, the body of the King by itself at the head of the tomb, the Queen at his feet, namely in the Choir before the High Altar, where even to-day they rest in magnificence." [1] Then follows an epitaph. Giraldus Cambrensis, whose works I have not seen, writing about 1192 A.D., gave an account of this opening of the tomb at which he was present. John of Glastonbury's account shows evidence of having come originally from someone present— the preparations round the spot, the Abbot giving the order to proceed, the much-worn monuments (which, doubtless, John saw himself later), the almost despair of the diggers, the test of the size of the gigantic tibia, the momentary view and then the crumbling of Guinevere's beautiful golden hair, the joy of the translation, the details of the laying of the Queen at the feet and not the side of the King in the new tomb.

He then gives us another scene eighty-eight years later, when the new Minster was finished, after Richard's Crusades and Simon de Montfort's Rebellions—the solemn keeping of Easter at Glaston by Edward I. and Queen Eleanor, and the Archbishop of Canterbury, when with great pomp and ceremony the new tomb was opened, and the remains placed in a finished shrine, the King and Queen assisting. Those who ask us to believe that all this is fable, instead of a scene in a fairly continuous history, ask us to believe that in the midst of the most solemn and holy Eastertide celebrations, the Abbot and assembled religious deliberately fooled the King and Queen and magnates of the realm, and acted a solemn and impious imposture. We want evidence and not surmise before believing in such slander. This is what he tells us; it is another scene in this long history to make the past live : "After these things in the beginning of the year of Our Lord 1278, on the Wednesday next before Easter, the Lord Edward the King in the sixth year of his reign, with the Lady Eleanor his wife, Queen of England, came to Glastonbury there to celebrate at their own expenses the said Easter. Where first the Lord King, and after the Lady Queen, were solemnly received separately with a procession."

Then follows an interesting account how the Earl Marshal's agents were not allowed to do the catering as "being against the liberties of their Church and of the

---

[1] Translated from Hearne's (small paper) Edition, pp. 182-3.

Twelve Hides " of Glaston, as " no man, king, archbishop, bishop, judge, sheriff, forester, or any bailiff or servant, or any man could perform any office in that liberty." Then he goes on : " On Maundy Thursday came Lord Robert, Archbishop of Canterbury, and he was received with a solemn procession after the hour of prime." Then follows a story of how the Archbishop made there a Holy Chrism, the Diocesan being away at that time in distant parts, and how the monks would not allow the Archdeacon of Wells to offer the oil and balsam, and how the Archbishop supported their contention that the monks should serve in their own Church. We are also told of an ordination of the King's Vice-Chancellor to the Diaconate, and of the King's Treasurer and two others to the priesthood on Easter Eve, and of the Archbishop pontificating[1] on Easter Day " as on the three preceding ones." The King had said that wherever he was on Easter Monday he would hold an Assize. But the Abbot and convent protested at what would have been an infringement of the liberties and immunities of the " Twelve Hides," and the King ordered the Assize to be held outside them at a village called Street. On the same day a certain Philip Cogan—(a suspiciously Irish name)—had a quarrel with the King's bodyguard, and drew a knife on them. He was immediately imprisoned for lèse majesté ! But the Abbot immediately released him, and amends were made through the Abbot's bailiffs. " On the Tuesday following, the King and the whole Court, after being entertained entirely at the expense of the Monastery, in the evening of the same day caused the tomb of the illustrious King Arthur to be opened, where in two coffins, with their likenesses and arms depicted, he finds separately the bones of the said King of an extraordinary size. But on the next day, that is Wednesday, the Lord King wrapping the bones of the King, and the Lady Queen the bones of the Queen in costly palls, shutting them in their own coffins, and sealing with their own seals, commanded the same sepulchre before the High Altar to be put together quickly, but the heads and faces of each to be left outside because of the people's devotion, and a writing of this sort to be placed inside : ' Here are the bones of the Most Noble King Arthur, which in the year 1275 of our Lord's Incarnation, on the 13th Calends of May, were here placed together through Lord Edward the illustrious King of England, there being present the Most Serene Eleanor, Consort of the same Lord King, and daughter of Lord Ferrand,

---

[1] Am I justified in translating " officium solempniter adimplevit " by " pontificated "? Good Friday is included.

King of Spain, Master William de Middultone, the Elect
of Norwich, Master Thomas de Beke, then Archdeacon of
Dorset, and Treasurer of the said Lord the King, the Lord
Henry de Lacey Earl of Lincoln, the Lord Amadius Count
of Savoy, and many other magnates of England.'" This
mention of the Count of Savoy is particularly interesting.
It was Amadius V. or Great who lived A.D. 1249-1323. He
is just one of the people whom no one would have thought
of naming, if he had not been present. He was a first
cousin of Eleanor of Provence, the mother of Edward I.
His uncle, Peter Count of Savoy, when his nieces became
the wives of Henry III. and of the King's brother Richard,
Earl of Cornwall, was made Earl of Richmond, and built
the Savoy Palace in London. The dates, too, of his
Easter week can all be tested to see whether they fit in
with Easter that year, and with the days of the week. So
also can be tested "the Elect of Norwich," and the
tenure of the two offices by Thomas de Beke. We
may claim that we have an account of a scene which
actually took place, and it is unthinkable that it was all
an impious fraud. I think that we may also claim that
we have a continuous history of the remains of Arthur,
which must have come originally from eye-witnesses of the
events recorded. May we not say that there was a motive
for the original silence about Arthur's grave, that simultaneously a Celtic history broke it to two Norman monks,
Geoffrey and William, that both indicated the date, manner
and place of Arthur's death, and the city of his burial ;
that one, a welcome habitué and finally adopted son of the
great Abbey, learnt and published the site of the very
unexpected spot where he was buried ; that about fifty
years after, in 1190, his tomb was opened and an account
was given, with details that suggest an eye-witness as the
original source, by John of Glastonbury, and that an actual
contemporary, Giraldus Cambrensis, who stated that he
was an eye-witness, also wrote an account within a very
few years' time. I think that we may say that King
Arthur and Queen Guinevere, stripped of all legend, lie
at Glastonbury. One wonders whether under the sward
their coffins remain undisturbed, when their great shrine
was swept away. The site of the old Altar, the one before
Abbot Monington's was built, is quite well-known.

But not merely does one believe Avalon to be the
grave of Arthur ; it is inseparably linked with his life. If
the Athelney of Alfred lies to the south-east of Glastonbury, surely the Camelot of Arthur lies to the south-west.
Glastonbury was the Royal Isle in the time of the Celtic

Kings, all through the Heptarchy, until and after Wessex
became Saxon England. Caliburn, Arthur's famous sword,
was forged at Glastonbury; he threw it away into the
River Brue by the famous Pomparles or Pons Perilous
Bridge, between Glastonbury and Street. If he was borne
to the mystic holy isle by water to die, how often in virile
manhood did he ride there ! The great fortified camp on
the top of the hill at South Cadbury, which Somerset
tradition has always linked with Arthur, is surely Camelot
of the Round Table.[1] At its feet lies the little village of
Queen Camel, and two miles further west the hamlet of
West Camel, and ancient inhabitants still recall Camelet
as one of the names of Cadbury Fort itself. To climb the
hill to this wondrous fortified camp is to realize its
impregnability and to drink in the air of romance.
Whether one goes when the steep lane leading to it is
clad with the white violets that speak of the erstwhile
blameless court, or when the sunshine of the primroses
or whole skies of bluebells deck its groves, or when the
leaves are ending their lives in a golden glory so typical
of Arthur, there is always the same magic charm. The
loftily-poised fort itself is situated on the extremity of a
range of hills. From its eastern side one still sees the
last battlefield between the victorious Saxon and the
stricken Celt. The views are amazing. It is an eagle's
eyrie. There are four deep concentric ditches and massive
ramparts enclosing some twenty acres. In the centre the
moated mound is called King Arthur's Palace. In the
fourth ditch there is a spring called King Arthur's Well.
Ancient weapons, camp equipment and a silver horse-shoe
have been dug up in it. Was it the shoe of Arthur's own
horse? Down in the valley to the north, between Bruton
and Ditcheat, there is a little bridge called Arthur's
Bridge, the name also of a little inn hard by. And the
tradition lingers that Arthur and his knights came by one
day when the stream was swollen and there was no ford,
and he ordered the bridge to be built. And within the
fort itself there is a Ride called King Arthur's Hunting
Ride, and it leads direct north-westward towards the
church-crowned Tor of Avalon.[2] Did he not live within
sight of Avalon, where he was to be buried, this most
Christian King? If this be not Camelot, what is it? If
this be not Arthur's, whose is it? Go and see it, and
as you gaze the answer will come to you. The ethereal
breezes on the top of this lofty hill are the very atmosphere
of Camelot and Arthur's court. Something will tell you,
and you will know. Yes; this is Camelot at last.

[1] In 1143 " pensiones " were allowed to the Almonry of the Abbey
from Camelarton and Middlezoy. Where was Camelarton?

[2] Right away on the other side of the valley on the Mendips above
Wells is " Arthur's Point."

There is little space here to discuss the stories of the Holy Grail, so inseparably associated with Arthur and Glastonbury. Suffice it to say that the earliest traced Continental sources are French. Not only did British Christianity and St. Joseph himself come *viâ* France, but the close association between Armorica (or Brittany) and Britain can scarcely be exaggerated. The British Royal Family and the Breton were one, so were the two peoples in origin. Before the invading Saxons, whole sections of the British Church with their Bishops fled to Brittany. All the three earliest Continental sources of the Holy Grail story were French. Chretien de Troyes wrote his Contes del Graal from a book given him by Comte Philippe de Flandres, 1185-9. In 1198-1210, Wolfram von Eschenbach wrote the German version, Parsifal. He quotes Chretien, but repudiates his story and claims for his own, a French origin, Kyot le Provencal, le Chanteur. That source is lost. And Robert le Barron, a Frenchman, wrote about 1204. So it is not at all hard to conceive that the story travelled from Glastonbury to the Continent viâ France.

And there is another consideration not to be neglected. The very time when these ballads of the Grail begin to be circulated in France, is the very time when the interest of Henry II. of England began to be awakened in the British King Arthur, and the search for his body was urged, and soon carried out. And it is not to be over-looked that Henry II. was not only King of England but the greatest ruler on the Continent. By marriage or inheritance his possessions were enormous. He actually reigned over far more of France that the King of France. Normandy, Anjou, Maine were his by descent, Poitou and Guienne by marriage with Eleanor of Aquitaine, and later Brittany came under his power. Thus the whole of the West of France from North to South was his. History names him as the one who re-awoke the fame of Arthur, and to his time, and to his dominions, are traced back the earliest songs of the Grail. It was the golden age of troubadours. Queen Eleanor, wife of Henry II., was one of their great patronesses, and she even protected Bernart of Ventadour when expelled for making love to the Vicomtesse de Ventadour. And Bertran de Born, the most famous of all troubadours, was active with tongue and pen in the wars between Henry and his rebel sons. At the Court of Henry the troubadours and their art, the revivified stories of Arthur at Avalon, and of the Holy Grail at Avalon, all met, and the stories elaborated and inter-mingled floated through Europe in the lays of the minstrel, and linger yet.   Modern powers of transit, and reproduction, make it more possible to seek the earlier sources of the stories.

The idylls that surround Arthur's name are such that he and his Court are a synonym for purity and chivalry. Hence without hesitation one includes him among the Saints of Avalon.

GILDAS, A.D. 516-570.

William of Malmesbury says that Gildas the Wise "spent many years" at Glastonbury, "charmed by the sanctity of the spot.   There, too, in the year of Our Lord 512 he passed out of this life, and lies buried in the Old Church before the Altar."   The date is certainly wrong ; else he died before he was born !   It is claimed, too, that he was buried in the Island of Horac, off Brittany, where he had been an Anchorite.   And we hear of his being an Anchorite on the Island of Steepholm, off Weston-super-Mare, and, being driven thence by pirates, he found a rest at Avalon and built a church to the Blessed Trinity by the banks of a stream.   William speaks very positively. He was careful and critical.   There could be no more fitting burial-place for the Celtic Gildas, the earliest known British historian, unless it were Llaniltud (or Llantwit), Major in Glamorganshire.   For there, in that rival of Glastonbury, like one of the " three Perpetual Choirs of Britain," which fell in the sixth century, he was born.   The College of Llaniltud itself was founded by St. Iltyd in the fifth century—(some say by St. Germanus under St. Iltyd) —and there St. Gildas, St. David, Bishop Paulinus of Leon, and Taliessin, Chief of the Bards, were brought up.

But Llan Ilid which adjoins it is older still in its history, that Church being dedicated to St. Ilid, who came with Aristobulus and Bran the father of Caractacus from Rome, and settled in Glamorganshire shortly after the coming of St. Joseph of Arimathea to Glaston.   It is claimed, as we shall see later,[1] that St. Iltyd himself, when the Danes were harrying Wales, was carried to the safe resting-place of Glastonbury.   It is most likely that Gildas, the Celtic scholar, would be attracted by the famous library and the sanctity of Glastonbury.   Perhaps there he learnt and revealed to us that Christianity came in the last year of Tiberius Cæsar, A.D. 37.   Where else could he so fittingly learn it ?   Perhaps there he told of the awful persecution under Diocletian, A.D. 300.   (He who first learnt it in his

[1] V. p. 50.

birthplace in earliest childhood as an awful memory. The
very Church of Llanharan, which also adjoins Llanilid, is
dedicated to Julius and Aaron, two of the priests who fell
in that time of horror.¹) Perhaps there, in that quiet
cloister, he revealed the insidious growth of the Arian
heresy. Perhaps there, with Celtic courage, he fearlessly
drew the picture of his own decadent times and decadent
Church. (We must make allowance for Celtic despondency
and pessimism which alternates with incurable optimism.
A disillusioned optimist is a most appalling pessimist).
Perhaps there he bravely charged the Celtic Church with
its crowning fault—that they never preached the truth to
the hated Saxon. Surely there he rests, his troubles at
an end, in the holiest spot in England. And there, at any
rate, Gildas was remembered in the Calendar of that
Church of Glastonbury² under the title of " St. Gildas the
Wise." R.I.P.

KING INA—Reigned a.d. 688-725,

AND

SAINT PAULINUS—Died a.d. 644.

How is it possible to leave out King Ina of Wessex
from the Saints of Glastonbury? He who was the first to
build a really great Church on to St. Joseph's, the fore-
runner of the present great ruined Church, in memory of
his brother Mules as we have seen.³ Son of King Cenred,
sixth in descent from Cerdic, he loved Glastonbury with
all the passion of his virile race. His famous laws, his
building of the great Minster, his munificent gifts to it,
his grants of privileges and lands, his abdication of his
regal state, and his departure with his Queen, Ethelburga,
to Rome, there to live in lowly guise and mean attire, and
there so to die—in other words, his justice, his zeal for
God, his generosity, his humility, all proclaim the Saint.

William of Malmesbury transcribes his first Privilege
to Glastonbury Abbey, which he confirmed in the "Wooden
Basilica," a.d. 704. This name for the Old Church is
particularly interesting, because William tells us elsewhere⁴
that " St. Paulinus, created Bishop of Rochester after
being Archbishop of York, so saith the tradition of the
fathers, improved the shell of the Church (for a long time,

¹ In Britain alone 6 Bishops and various priests, and over 10,000
communicants were martyred.
² Dean Robinson's " The Times of Dunstan," pp. 102-3.
³ V. p. 26.
⁴ C. 19.

as we have said, composed of rushes), by covering it with wooden panelling and with lead from top to bottom. So great indeed was his skill in that work that he took from the Church none of its sanctity, while he increased its beauty in many ways." [1]

The Dean of Wells draws attention to the fact that St. Paulinus appears in the Glastonbury Calendar,[2] which is a little surprising. When Edwin King of Northumbria wanted to marry Ethelburga, daughter of King Ethelbert of Kent, he was at first refused as being a pagan, but promising her freedom of religion, the marriage was consented to, and Paulinus was consecrated Bishop, and sent with her. Eumer, an envoy from the King of Wessex, treacherously tried to kill Edwin by stabbing on Easter Day A.D. 625. The King's life was saved through Lilla, a faithful Thane, thrusting himself between the King and the assassin. Lilla was killed, the dagger passing right through his breast and wounding Edwin. The shock caused the premature confinement of the Queen. and the life of herself and her babe were in danger. The prayers of Paulinus saved the mother and child, and the latter was baptized on Whit Sunday. Edwin set off to punish Wessex. Ere he went he vowed that if he were successful he would be baptized. He returned victorious, and after some hesitation, he and many of his family and nation were baptized on Easter Day, 627.

I tell the story, as it shows some intercourse between Wessex and Northumbria in Paulinus's day. And it must be remembered that Glastonbury's sacred fame drew many into Wessex. The Dean points out that the inclusion in the Glastonbury Calendar of St. Paulinus of York,[3] and the fact that William of Malmesbury, who saw the Old Church, must have seen that its appearance indicated the truth of the timbering story, suggests the truth of his story that Paulinus went to Glastonbury and performed this labour of love.

It is also curious to note that in this " First Privilege" Ina speaks of the Olde Church as the Church of the Blessed Mother of God, Mary, and the Blessed Patrick.[4] In 719 he built on to it the Church of St. Peter and St. Paul. "The said King also caused to be constructed a chapel of gold and silver, with ornaments and vessels of the same,

---

[1] Lomax' Translation.
[2] V. later p. 52.
[3] Afterwards Bishop of Rochester, when with Queen Ethelburga he fled back to Kent after Edwin's assassination.
    It is quite probable that St. David dedicated his chancel to St. Patrick, or St. Mary and St. Patrick. V. pp. 24-27.

below the greater Church. To do so he gave 2,640 pounds
of silver, and the Altar was composed of 264 pounds of
gold, the chalice and paten of 10 pounds of gold, the censer
of 8 pounds, and 10 mancuses[1] of gold; candelabra of
12½ pounds of silver; covers for the Books of the Gospel,
20 pounds and 60 mancuses of gold; water-vessel and
another Altar-vessel of 17 pounds of gold; foot-baths of
eight pounds of gold; vessel for Holy water of 20 pounds
of silver; figure of the Lord and the Blessed Virgin and the
Twelve Apostles of 175 pounds of silver and 38 pounds of
gold; an Altar-cloth and sacerdotal ornaments, cunningly
interwoven everywhere with gold and precious stones. All
this treasure the said King gave devoutly to the Monastery
of Glastonbury out of honour for the Holy Mother of God
and Virgin Mary. Moreover, he confirmed her lands,
possessions and liberties to the Church by a royal document
in these words."[2] Then follows a Charter of the Church.
This is given by the advice of his Queen Sexburga and of
Berthwald, Archbishop of Canterbury (formerly Abbot of
Glastonbury, and later of Reculver), and of others. It
quotes his predecessor, King Kentwin, "who used to call
Glastonbury 'the Mother of Saints,' and liberated it from
every secular and ecclesiastic service, and granted it this
dignified privilege, that the brethren of that place should
have the power of electing and appointing their ruler
according to the rule of St. Benedict." It goes on to for-
bid " all princes, archbishops, bishops, dukes and governors
of my kingdom, as they tender my honour and regard, and
all dependents, mine as well as theirs as they value their
personal safety, never to dare to enter the island of Our
Lord Jesus Christ and of the eternal Virgin of Glastonbury,
nor the possession of the said Church, for the purpose of
holding courts, making inquiry, or seizing, or doing anything whatever to the offence of the servants of God there
residing; moreover, I particularly inhibit by the curse of
Almighty God, of the eternal Virgin Mary, and of the Holy
Apostles Peter and Paul, and of the rest of the Saints, any
bishop on any account whatever from presuming to take his
episcopal seat or celebrate Divine service, or consecrate
Altars, or dedicate Churches, or do anything whatever,
either in the Church of Glastonbury itself or its dependent
Churches, that is to say, Sowy, Brente, Merlinch, Sapewic,
Stret, Sbudeclalech, Pilton,[3] or in their chapel or islands,
unless he be specially invited by the Abbot or brethren of

---

[1] 55 grains, Troy weight.
[2] De Antiquitate, C. 40.
[3] Sowy, Brent, Moorlinch, Shapwick, Street, Butleigh, Pilton.

that place." [1] Whether we think this amazing Charter genuine or not, it shows what the claims of Glastonbury were, at least in the Middle Ages, as we learn elsewhere. Of the places named, Moorlinch, Shapwick, Street, and Butleigh are to-day in the Jurisdiction of Glastonbury. Baltonsborough, Burtle, Catcott, Chilton Polden, Edington, Godney, Meare, Middlezoy, Othery, Walton, West Pennard and Western Zoyland, which are within it to-day are omitted. This may help to give the latest date for the Charter. Probably there were no Churches there. It is also of note that of all the places named in the Charter, Pilton is the only one situated within the Twelve Hides, and that this is to-day outside of the jurisdiction of Glastonbury, probably an arbitrary transfer to another Rural Deanery. Either the Church of Pilton was the only Church in the Twelve Hides other than the Glastonbury Churches at the date of the Charter, or else the Churches in the Twelve Hides were purposely omitted as being covered by the words " the Church of Glastonbury," and Pilton was put in for a special reason. It might be that the boundary goes right through the middle of the Church of Pilton, or the reason might be that the Charter goes on to say that two mansions out of the Church of Glastonbury's possessions were put aside, that when the Bishop came or went at the Abbot's invitation he might have a place of entertainment, viz., one in Pilton and one in Poelt. The one at Pilton is close to the Church, and the Church itself, as stated above, is half in the Twelve Hides, and half not. The limitations to the use of these mansions are worth quoting : " Nor shall it be lawful to him " (the Bishop), "even to pass the night here, unless he be detained by stress of weather or bodily sickness, or invited by the Abbot or monks, and then with not more than three or four clerks" ! Verily, the Bishop was kept in order. And more was to come : "Moreover, let the aforesaid Bishop be mindful every year with his clerks that are at Wells, to acknowledge his Mother Church of Glastonbury with Litanies on the second day after Our Lord's Ascension, and should he haughtily defer it, or fail in the things which are above recited and confirmed, he shall forfeit his mansions above mentioned." He no longer needs the mansions. He may come and go as he pleases. The Litanies are not said. Such is the decay of godly custom and discipline, and the haughtiness of Bishops ! Even the Mother that begat them is slighted and neglected ! To return to Ina himself. He was a munificent bestower of lands over a long period to the

[1] Lomax' translation of De Antiquitate, pp. 79-80.

Church of Glastonbury. In A.D. 690, when Hemgislus was Abbot, he bestowed Brent ten hides ; in A.D. 705, when Berwold was Abbot, 20 hides close to Tamer, Sowy 12 hides, Pilton 20 hides, Doulting 20 hides ; in A.D. 719, when Echfrid was Abbot, one hide with fishing rights on the Axe—probably Bledenhida. He also confirmed, and probably increased, the Abbot's enormous judicial powers within the Twelve Hides : " And whatsoever question shall arise, whether of homicide, sacrilege, poison, theft, rapine, the disposal and jurisdiction of Churches, the ordination of clerks ecclesiastical synods, and all judicial inquiries, they shall be determined by the decision of the Abbot and convent without the interference of any person whatever." [1]

It was King Ina, too, who made the submission of the Church of Glastonbury and of himself to Rome between A.D. 725 and A.D. 728. He first sent letters under the Royal Seal, together with costly gifts to the Pontiff, entreating that " the Pope should receive the Church of Glastonbury with its appurtenances and properties into the protection of the Holy Roman Church, and should confirm the same in perpetuity by his apostolic authority." [2] The same year the King went to Rome, and fetched away the Privilege under the Apostolic Seal, and deposited it at Glastonbury. Thus, nearly 700 years after its foundation, and over 100 years after the Roman Mission under St. Augustine, the fons et origo of the Great British Celtic Church by an isolated act became in union with Rome. King Ina with his Queen went to Rome the same year, and died there as a humble man. He is buried in Rome, not in Wells as many think, misled by a stone in the nave of Wells Cathedral, giving his name and date, which unimaginatively is supposed to convey that Ina built a Church on that spot.

ST. TECLA, OR ST. THECLA.

EIGHTH CENTURY.

St. Tecla was a Virgin and Abbess,[3] one of the little band of brave and pious women invited by St. Boniface, alias St. Winfred, the great saint, who converted Germany, to educate Christian nuns there. She was doubtless named after the great St. Thecla of Apostolic days, the friend of St. Paul. The British Church always looked to the East. I have inserted her name among the

[1] De Antiquitate (Lomax), C. 40.
[2] De Antiquitate (Lomax), C. 41.
[3] At Kitzingen on the Maine (Greswell's Dumnonia p. 95.)

better known saints as there are little shreds of evidence
which, if pieced together, throw a light on what Glastonbury was in early days.　She is one of a multitude whose
association with Glastonbury has been forgotten.　There
is a tiny island in the Severn named after St. Tecla.　The
ancient name of Street, the townlet separated from the
Isle of Avalon or Glastonbury by the River Brue and
Pomparles Bridge, the early Roman Bridge, sacred to
King Arthur's memory,[1] was Lantokay or Lantokal.　Llan
is Church.　Tokal is metathesis for Thecla.[2]　Now we
know that St. Boniface was a Dumnonian, and that
Dumnonia included Devon and, at any rate, much of
Somerset, probably as far as the Parret or Axe.[3]　It was
Bishop Hedde who gave Llantokal to Glastonbury in
A.D. 681.　There exists a letter from St. Boniface, who
was trained at Exeter (Escan Ceaster),[4] fifty miles from
Glastonbury, to the Mother Superior of a convent on
Wirral or Weary All Hill, the hill where tradition says
that St. Joseph of Arimathea and his comrades landed.
But for this letter, and the story of King Arthur's vision,[5]
we should not know of the existence of this convent.　At
the foot of Weary All is the River Brue.　And about 400
yards off is Street Parish Church, now dedicated to the
Holy Trinity, but once apparently called Tecla's Church—
Llantokal.　So here we have almost forgotten information
and names that link to the neighbourhood of Glastonbury
the great St. Boniface of Germany and his disciple, St.
Tecla.　Nor is this all.　There is a lingering place name
which points to St. Tecla.　Some 50-60 years ago, Mr.
Maundrell, of Bove Town, tells me, the boys of Chilkwell
Street (Chalice Well Street) were wont to resort to the
orchard on Chalice Hill, now owned by Mr. R. T. Gould,
as a favourite playing ground.　They called it, without
knowing why, Stickler's Cross.　There are no cross-
roads, or any road at all there.　The name is probably
a corruption of St. Tecla's Cross.　From this site you
could have looked down into the valley at St. Tecla's
Church at Street.　The name of St. Tecla probably
remains elsewhere in the Celtic Church—at Llan Degla,
near Mold, in the diocese of St. Asaph, and at Coatfree,
in Brittany, there is a church dedicated to her, as Mr.
Joseph Clark, of Street, tells me.　Saints Thecla,
Margaret and Catherine were depicted on the walls of

---

[1] V. p. 40.
[2] V. Som. Arch. Proceedings for 18—, Vol. —, pp. —
[3] Greswell's " History of Glastonbury Abbey," p. 66.
[4] Or possibly Axbridge.
　　V. p. 32. n.

Cleeve Abbey in Somerset, but whether that St. Thecla is the local saint or the convert of St. Paul I know not. She was probably the latter—a trio of Eastern saints, from one of whom our Thecla took her name.

St. Boniface was martyred A.D. 755. So we get an approximate date for the Somerset St. Tecla. Lantokay was given to Glastonbury by Bishop Hedde with the consent of Kings Kentwin and Baldred somewhere about 680. It was apparently called Leghe then, a name which still lingers.

Before leaving this subject it is worth noting that after St. Gildas had been driven by pirates from the Island of Steepholme, off the coast of Somerset, he came and settled at Glastonbury and built himself a cell and a chapel hard by, dedicated to the High and Undivided Trinity, beside a stream.[1] Was this on the site of the present Parish Church of Street, which is dedicated to the Holy Trinity? Did St. Tecla build a large church there, keeping the same dedication? There are many pieces of Roman pottery dug up close to Street Church and in the churchyard earlier than A.D. 401 ; so there was a little Roman colony there. The question becomes more complicated because Street Church once had a dedication to St. Giles or St. Gildas. Mr. Joseph Clark tells me it is written in a MS. "St. Gild—."

John of Glastonbury, Hearne's Edition, pp. 73-74, says that after the Abbot of Glastonbury had gladly received him, "the most religious Gildas again desired to lead the life of a hermit, and departing by the river's bank near Glastonbury, he built a Church to the Holy and Undivided Trinity called the Chapel of Happy Retreat." There he died.

John of Glastonbury goes on : "and with much mourning and great honour he was buried in the Old Church, A.D. 512. Moreover, on that spot where he lived a hermit's life is now a Parish Church dedicated in the name of this saint." As the Church of Street appears to have used both dedications—to the Holy Trinity and St. Gildas—and to have been called Tecla's Church, can it be that St. Gildas, who died in 512, built the first chapel here to the Holy Trinity, that St. Tecla built a larger one with the same dedication, or possibly to the Holy Trinity and Gildas, and that the whole hamlet was called Tecla's Church, while the church itself kept its dedication? Are the blazing buttercups which deck in spring the little stream which separates Llantokal or Street from Avalon or Glastonbury so brilliant because

[1] V. p. 42.

they are halos of these two saints—the historian hermit and the brave, frail woman whose zeal carried her to distant Germany? Under the lee of St. Joseph's Hill, in sight of the church-crowned Tor with all that it stands for, hard by the ancient bridge, and the Roman, if not British, road which led through the swamp from the Holy Isle to what had been the little settlement of Roman potters, these saints chose their sites well. Do their spirits ever wander in these golden meads so little trodden still by men? It is a walk of wondrous peace still.

VARIOUS TRANSLATED SAINTS.

St. Iltud of Glamorganshire, Fifth Century.
St. Aidan of Lindisfarne, d. A.D. 651.
St. Hilda of Whitby, A.D. 614-680.
St. Benedict Bishop, 7th and 8th Century.
Venerable Bede, A.D. 673-735.
St. Ceolfrid, living A.D. 710.

It is claimed that to protect them from the ravages of heathen invaders, or to satisfy the perverted veneration of Christian invaders, all these were translated at one time or another to the repose of Glastonbury. What a company of earth's really mighty ones! The Celtic *St. Iltud*, scholar and founder of a great college early in the fifth century, of whom we have already written somewhat, who is said to have known St. Germanus of Auxerre, and is called by William of Malmesbury "St. Iltuit, glorious among the Welsh." *St. Aidan* of Lindisfarne, who, after the death of Edwin of Northumbria in A.D. 633,[1] and the return to Kent of St. Paulinus, Archbishop of York, with Ethelburga (Edwin's widowed Queen, a Kentish princess), was sent from Iona to Northumbria in A.D. 634 at Oswy's request to reconvert it. Thus came the stream of Celtic Christianity to the North viâ Glastonbury to Ireland, Ireland to Iona, Iona to Northumbria, stamping a Celtic impression on the Northern Church until the days of Wilfrid. *St. Hilda* of Whitby, A.D. 614-680, niece of the above King Edwin, baptized by the above Paulinus in the first flush of his triumphant missionary zeal. She fled with her aunt and Paulinus to Kent after her uncle's murder. Recalled by the above St. Aidan, St. Paulinus' successor in the North, she became Abbess of Hartlepool, and finally founded Whitby Abbey where, with amazing success she ruled both monks and nuns. *St. Benedict Bishop,* Abbot of Wearmouth and then Jarrow, reputed to be the first man

[1] Killed in battle, together with his son Osfrid, by Cadwalla and Penda.

to introduce large stone buildings and glass windows into Britain, founder of a great Church library, to whom was entrusted the tuition of Bede at the early age of seven. He is said to sleep here with his successor Ceolfrid, and his pupil Bede, all from the far away North. *Bede, the Venerable Bede,* born at Wearmouth in A.D. 673, in the territory of its Abbey, brought up at that Abbey from tender years under Benedict Bishop and Ceolfrid, transferred to Jarrow Abbey at ten years old, made a Dean at nineteen, and a priest at thirty. He refused the Abbacy that he might not be hindered in his literary work, and wrote over forty treatises, and was still writing when, at 58, he died and was buried at Jarrow, and was moved by St. Cuthbert to Durham, where in the twelfth century Bishop Pudsey put up to him a shrine which was destroyed by Henry VIII. Does he really sleep at the Southern Minster of which he apparently never heard? Who brought these people from the North? Aidan the Celt, Hilda the Northumbrian, he who summoned her, princess though she was, from Southern Kent, and she came obedient to work together in that bleak North, and then in death to meet in drowsy, mellow Avalon! Aidan and Wilfrid, too, champions respectively of the Celtic and the Roman Church in the distant North, the former to be borne here in death, where there is reason to believe that Wilfrid at least once came in life! Benedict Bishop, too, who voyaged in Wilfrid's youth, with him to sunny Rome! It is whispered that after life's voyage ended Benedict Bishop sleeps here, where his comrade Wilfrid once trod in the flesh. How comes it? The present Dean of Wells has so well put the problem[1] that we will answer in his words : "Two other entries occur[2] with the addition of the words 'in Glaston.' These are St. Aidan the Bishop, and St. Ceolfrid the Abbot. The latter was the great Abbot of Jarrow and Wearmouth for whom the famous Codex Amiatinus of the Vulgate was written. How came Glastonbury to make the audacious claim that these Saints from the far North rested in her burial ground? We turn again to William of Malmesbury. 'When the Danes,' he says, 'were ravaging Northumbria, a certain Abbot Tica took refuge at Glastonbury, and was made Abbot there in 754. He brought with him relics of St. Aidan and the bodies of Ceolfrid, Benedict (Biscop), and other Abbots of Wearmouth ; also of Bede the Presbyter and Abbess Hilda.' Another tradition said that these Saints were sent to Glas-

[1] " The Times of St. Dunstan," pp. 101-2-3.
[2] In the Glastonbury Calendar in the Bosworth Psalter, v. pp. 15-6.

tonbury by King Edmund, when on his northern expedition.
This was, of course, when Dunstan was the Abbot.
William of Malmesbury, in his various writings, wavers
between these two explanations, but. he seems to have
decided ultimately for the earlier date (Som. Hist. Essays,
pp. 19-f.) Our Calendar tells us, at any rate, that in
St. Dunstan's time Aidan and Ceolfrid were certainly believed to lie at Glastonbury. For St. Aidan we can cite
two other early authorities. The first is the English tract
on the Resting-places of the Saints, which Lieberman
published in 1889. This collection was begun, he tells us,
before 995, and completed between 1013 and 1030. Here
we read ' There rest in Glastonbury St. Aidan and St.
Patrick, and many other Saints.' The second witness is
the Old English Martyrology, of which we have one small
fragment that goes back to c.850. Of the two full copies,
one was written in the first half, the other in the second
half of the tenth century. The earlier copy says of St.
Aidan : ' His bones are half of them in Scotland (or
Scottum), half in St. Cuthbert's Minster.' But the later
copy has for the second part of the sentence : ' half at
Glastonbury in St. Mary's Minster.' The alteration would
be in harmony with the tradition that ' relics of St. Aidan '
—(not the whole body, be it noted)—' came south as late
as King Edmund's time,' But it is quite possible a Glastonbury monk, in making the correction, wished to assert
a very ancient claim of his Abbey. We are not here con-
cerned with the truth of the tradition, but with the early
date to which it can be taken back ; for myself, however,
I see no reason to question the truth of it in one or other
of its forms . . .   Two other names we will pick out
before we leave this Calendar, St. Paulinus, Bishop of
Rochester, and St. Wilfrid, Bishop. . . . As to St.
Wilfrid, that wandering prelate is said by his biographer
to have visited King Centwine of the West Saxons, and
to have been the friend of King Caedwalla, who made him
gifts of lands. A Glastonbury Charter said that King
Centwine gave him Wedmore, and it was believed that the
Abbey had afterwards received it and lost it again. Here,
at any rate, we have an explanation of his somewhat
unexpected mention in our Calendar."

The Dean does not claim that St. Wilfrid
sleeps at Glastonbury, but he finds that St. Wilfrid
was commemorated here in St. Dunstan's time, he
finds in that Saint's biography the record of visits to
Wessex and its Kings, Centwine and Caedwalla, and he
finds in a Glastonbury Charter the gift of Wedmore to him

by King Centwine, and apparently by him to the Abbey.[1]
It was King Centwine who called Glastonbury "The
Mother of Saints."

ST. DUNSTAN.

Last, most English, and perhaps the greatest of all
the Saints of Glastonbury canonized by the unbroken
Catholic Church, was Dunstan. Wherever he now lies, of
which we shall treat later on, to Glastonbury he belonged
in life through and through. Born at Glastonbury, about
four miles out, within the Twelve Hides and Parish of
Glastonbury, in what is now called Baltonsborough (Bals-
bury), where the Church is dedicated to him, he was brought
up as a boy by the monks (including Irish ones) at Glastonbury. He was a monk there, Abbot there, and what we
should now call Prime Minister there under Edmund the
Magnificent and Edgar the Peaceable, both of which kings
lie buried within the Abbey. (King Edgar's palace was at
Edgarley, on the site of the Manor House, within Glastonbury Parish.) West of "The Old Church," and outside of it
are the foundations of St. Dunstan's Chapel, built very
probably over his workshop with a forge, where he had
his imaginary conflict with the Devil. Still further West,
on the other side of the modern wall, the house built within
the old Abbey walls is called St. Dunstan's, marking the
tradition of his vanished chapel, some of the foundations
of which were dug for and discovered a few years back in
the Abbey grounds, and some of which are probably in
the garden on the other side of the wall. One of the
greatest of Englishmen—like Alfred the Great and Nelson
—he suffered from epilepsy. Although the Anglo-Saxon
Chronicle says that he was born in A.D. 925—(a date
which it is believed was added in later but ancient days)—
events at which he was undoubtedly present prove that he
must have been born earlier, and Dean Armitage Robinson's date of A.D. 909, which accords with the views of
some other writers, makes everything fit into its place.
He was of royal descent, like so many other Abbots of the
Royal Isle of Glastonbury in Celtic, Saxon, and Norman
days. He was a nephew of Archbishop Athelm of Canterbury, and kinsman—and some say nephew—of Alphege the
Bald, Bishop of Winchester, both of which men played a
moulding part in his early life. Athelm commended him
to the notice of their mutual kinsman, King Athelstan,

[1] William of Malmesbury definitely says (De Antiquitate, Cap 39),
"Bishop Wilfred gave the Isle of Wethmore 70 hides, which had been
given to him by King Kenwin, and Cliwere Estate 1 hide."

at whose cultured and powerful court thronged by foreign princes, rulers to be, he drank in his first taste of politics, and Alphege persuaded and almost coerced him to be a monk. Dunstan was not only a man of extraordinary genius, but of the most versatile parts. He was not only distinguished in religion and politics, but in literature and the arts. No mean craftsman, he excelled in bell-making, clock-making, and in finer and ornamental metal work, and was a distinguished draughtsman. All the fine arts and embellishments of life were his, and he left his mark on his great Abbey in these as well as in religion and discipline. He founded the bell-making and clock-making for which Glastonbury Abbey was so famous. The three great existing clocks at Wells and Exeter Cathedrals and Wimborne Minster were all turned out at Glastonbury Abbey workshop by the monk Peter Lightfoot in the fourteenth century, and in the Bodleian Library is a wonderful drawing with masterly outline showing St. Dunstan at the feet of Christ, attributed to the Saint himself. He excelled in missal painting, and encouraged literature. He was so much too clever for his contemporaries that he was accused of wizardry even as a young man. Jealousy and annoyance probably prompted this too, for the youth was a great favourite with the ladies of Athelstan's court. But probably the main factor was the age-long dislike of the uncultured for anything which they cannot understand.

Excessive study as a boy brought about brain-fever in Dunstan. He narrowly escaped with his life, and his illness probably stimulated the visions of his later life. The dislike above mentioned brought about another and later attack. For a time the charge of wizardry had driven him from the Court. But he was soon back again in full favour, exercising his gifts and magnetic charm. Stirred up by these, his rougher companions waylaid him, ill-treated him, bound him and threw him in a pitiful condition in the marsh near Glastonbury, and left him there. He succeeded in escaping, and took refuge with his kinsman Bishop Alphege of Winchester, who had been appointed to that See about A.D. 934. There another attack of brain-fever almost finished him. And the Bishop, working upon his feelings, and persuading him to renounce a fair young girl of the Court to whom he was devotedly attached, with difficulty persuaded him to become a monk. This occurred about A.D. 936.—And he entered the cloister where he had been schooled as a boy.

This renunciation doubtless coloured his mind in the great dispute which was to occur under his archiepiscopate, and made him side with the celibacy of the clergy. But does not the severe wrench also account for his personal tenderness in not ousting the married clergy in his own Diocese, but letting them gradually die out?

About three years after his entering Glastonbury as a monk, King Athelstan died, and was succeeded by his younger brother, Edmund the Magnificent. The Court was often at Glastonbury, and Dunstan was found in intercourse with the King, but he was soon plotted against, and again banished from the Court, but not without qualms of conscience on the part of the King. Then followed a most romantic incident. No one can fully appreciate it who has not seen the glorious Cheddar Gorge, near Glastonbury and Wells. The King was entertaining a foreign prince, and they were hunting the wild stags in the Mendips. Their quarry made for the gorge, sprung over it, and was dashed to pieces. The hounds followed to a like fate. The King was close to them, and suddenly saw his peril. Death was imminent. Into his mind rushed his injustice to his young kinsman Dunstan, and he vowed a vow that if he were spared he would re-instate him. Contrary to all human expectation, his horse swerved on the very verge, and the King was saved. Then and there he immediately sought Dunstan, and proceeded with him to Glastonbury, and there nominated him Abbot at the age of about thirty-one of the greatest Abbey in the kingdom. The Abbacy must have been vacant. Perhaps it was for fear of the very appointment that Dunstan's enemies had been active. Thus came about the appointment of this man, forced as it were into monasticism, who was to revive and develop this form of religious life which was destined to play so active a part in the life of this country for six hundred years. Before long Dunstan was appointed Treasurer of the Kingdom, the first of England's great ecclesiastic statesmen, and had refused the Bishopric of Crediton which, like Wells, had been created a few years before his birth, in A.D. 905, out of older bishoprics.

In A.D. 946 King Edmund was assassinated at Pucklechurch, seven miles from Bristol, which for centuries belonged to Glastonbury Abbey, and had been the abode of St. Aldhelm. The King had gone there to celebrate the feast of St. Augustine, and in the middle of the banquet looked up and espied an outlaw, Leof, who had not only dared to enter, but was seated at the table. It is an insight into the man and into the manners of the day that, fired with indignation, the King rose in person, struggled with the intruder, and successfully threw him to the ground.

But as he lay under, the outlaw drew his dagger and mortally wounded the King.[1]

Edmund was succeeded by his brother Edred, who was sick during the greater part of his reign, and the kingdom was virtually ruled by Dunstan. Edred only reigned nine years, and was succeeded by his nephew Edwy, the son of Edmund. Edwy was a hot-headed youth who, encouraged by his mother, was determined on marrying his kinswoman, Elgiva, who was within the prohibited degrees. On this marriage of course the Church put her ban. It is the age-long struggle of man's lust against God's will. And as the Jewish Church had its Samuels, Elijahs, and Nathans, so has the Christian always had and always will have its St. John Baptists (belonging to both Churches), its St. Dunstans, and its Wolseys. And men of the world liking rulers of easy morality, who do not sit too heavily on their own easy consciences, generally side with the rulers and misinterpret the Saint. In Haydn's list of the Kings and Queens of England it is under Edwy alone that there is this sort of comment : " In this reign Dunstan, a turbulent and ambitious priest, ruled the King, who afterwards banished him." " A turbulent and ambitious priest !" A generous and courageous man of God, who gave up his own will, a man who had conquered himself and could stand up to others, a man of whom this was written : " Not a hair's breadth," he declared, " would he move from the law of his Lord.'"[2] So much is the verdict of history worth ! On Edwy's very coronation day we get an insight again into the times and into Dunstan the man, trained and valued in the Court of Edmund the man. Edwy had insulted the Witan, and outraged the Church by leaving the banqueting table and going to the blandishments of Elgiva, which they dreaded. The Witan wanted a spokesman, and Dunstan rose from the table, followed the King, and unceremoniously and perhaps physically forced him to return. He was never forgiven. He was soon outlawed, and fled to the Court of his kinsman Arnulf, Count of Flanders. There he entered a Benedictine Monastery at Ghent at the time when the Benedictine rule was surging over Europe. Thus, a third time without any accident, this rough-hewn piece of English oak was forced into surroundings which should enormously mould his country's future. Edwy's work was done. He had driven the great statesman-ecclesiastic to a new school. And he only reigned four years. He had been raised up for a purpose, as all scourges are. He was succeeded by

[1] Dunstan buried Edmund at Glastonbury.
[2] Dean Armitage Robinson's " The Times of St. Dunstan," p. 89.

a totally different man, Edgar the Peaceful. But before this came about, at the end of two years Mercia and Northumbria revolted from him and declared Edgar King, and in two years' time Edwy's death made Edgar King of all England. Then began a time of building up, with Dunstan as master mason. Edgar the same year appointed him Archbishop of Canterbury. The wholesome Benedictine rule which made each monastery self-supporting through its industries, and taught the people arts, forestry, husbandry, built great sea barriers and causeways, relieved the poor, nursed the sick, housed and fed the wayfarer, administered discipline, and curbed the power of lay tyrants, grew and flourished. Archbishop Dunstan did not so much take an active part as encourage, licence, and occasionally restrain others equally ardent, notably his old companion in the Glastonbury cloister, St. Ethelwold, Bishop of Winchester. King Edgar was as keen on monasticism as Dunstan. A synod held at Winchester resulted in a code called the Regularis Concordia, which laid down the details for practice of the Benedictine rule throughout the kingdom. This was issued in the King's name, and the King and Queen became protectors and supervisors—later called " Visitors "—for monasteries and nunneries respectively.[1] When Edgar the Peaceful was laid to rest in his beloved Glastonbury Abbey, in a pillar at the threshold of the Church[2]—(he was afterwards removed to a shrine over the Altar)[3]—Dunstan gave himself more and more to his religious duties. But his courage and far-seeing wisdom as a statesman are exemplified by two things. First, England was unified under Edgar through Dunstan, just as he had unified the monastic rule. Unity was his guiding star. Secondly, after Dunstan the deluge. There was no one to resist the Danes, and they over-ran the kingdom. Such was Glastonbury's and Somerset's greatest son, single-hearted, lion-hearted, God-fearing, versatile, wide of view. A great ecclesiastic, a great statesman, master of all arts, he loved little children and the poor. He had great spiritual gifts, and he was canonized almost immediately after his death, which took place in A.D. 988.

St. Dunstan was buried at Canterbury, where a shrine was put up to him, part of which remains. Does he lie there or at Glastonbury ? This is an age-long controversy between the two monasteries. William of Malmesbury's

---

[1] V. Dean Robinson's " The Times of St. Dunstan," pp. 88 and 89.
[2] De Antiquitate, C. 55.
[3] De Antiquitate, C. 59.

De Antiquitate devotes the whole of Chapters 23, 24 and 25 to the story of the Saint's translation to Glastonbury in A.D. 1012, after Canterbury Cathedral had been razed to the ground by the Danes and Kent ravaged up to the City of London itself, its inhabitants murdered, tortured, beaten or sold to slavery, and its buildings burnt, St. Alphege, the Archbishop, being himself imprisoned, tormented and, finally, murdered. A marginal note in the same hand as the text tells us that it is recorded in the life of St. Alphege that out of a population of 8,000 only four monks remained alive and only 800 " of the inferior order," and that these were later decimated and ill-treated. Edmund Ironside, who virtually and perhaps actually ruled with his weak father, and afterwards shared the kingdom with the Danish King Canute seven months, and was then murdered, was himself taken prisoner and ill-treated. Later he came to Glastonbury and stayed some time, and told the monks the story of the devastation, and of his own sufferings.[1] He expatiated, too, on St. Dunstan's great love for his native Glastonbury and the Abbey, his Alma Mater. This fired the monks with a desire to rescue and bring home his remains. They consulted the King, who gave his consent. The monks then chose four of their number, apparently the four survivors mentioned in the marginal note referred to above, for they were four monks who had undergone the miseries of the devastation at Canterbury. They were originally sons of Glastonbury, had gone with Dunstan to Canterbury to wait on him and perform the services of his chapel, and had actually helped to bury him. They had remained on at Canterbury, and had also ministered to St. Alphege later in his imprisonment and martyrdom, St. Alphege also being a son of Glastonbury Abbey. The names of these four are given us : Sebricht, Ethelbricht, Bussius and Adelworde, surnamed " Quadrens," which Mr. Lomax very happily translates " Tubby." This human touch of the nickname lingering on at Glastonbury long after his death—Tubby Adelworde—has its evidential value. They set out ; they found Canterbury desolate ; "they went without pausing to the sepulchre of the most holy man, well known to them who had themselves placed him in the tomb. When they had opened it, they found the bones of St. Dunstan lying upon gold and precious tapestry, the flesh after so long a space being all dissipated, and they began to gather together what they found as reverently as was fit, not without tears ; they recognised the ring, too, which had been placed upon the finger of the Saint when he was borne to burial, which, 'twas said, he had made himself at a tender

[1] He, too, was buried in Glastonbury Abbey.

age. Having, therefore, completed the object for which
they set out, returning infinite thanks for their prosperous
journey they return to Glastonbury, bearing joyfully with
them the precious relics.'' [1]   This mention of the ring made
by the Saint in his earlier days before the great cares of
Church and State came upon him, and put upon his finger
when he was laid to rest, is again a touch of local colour.
True, if these sons of Glastonbury had tended him to the
last, and helped to bury him, this ring might well have
been known of at Glaston, and not been necessarily discovered at the time of the opening of his grave.   But this
would be an evidence to the actual existence of these four
monks.   And that is something towards the truth of the
story.   Granting their existence, who so likely not merely
to be chosen but to promote such an enterprise?   It is a
most terrible supposition that whole communities of men
devoted to the religious life were wholesale liars and
forgers.   For this is something more than the chronicling
of pedigrees of patrons, which they were not able, or had
not troubled to investigate.   To publish a modern peerage
is not the same thing as deliberately and solemnly before
God to declare what you know to be the figment of your
own brain, and blasphemously to venerate with sacred
rites relics which you know to be absent.   A few individuals
are capable even of this, but not whole communities.   But
to go on.   Having got the relics, we are told, the monks
naturally feared the claiming again by Canterbury, should
that See again be restored to power, of the remains which
from the beginning the monks of Glastonbury would so fain
have had with them.   They therefore chose the two most
discreet senior monks to be the sole guardians of the secret
where they had laid their beloved Father at Glaston.   Only
when one was about to depart this life was the secret to
be disclosed to one other equally carefully chosen, he only
to disclose it under the same circumstances, and so on in
perpetuum, or until the time came when the secret could be
safely disclosed.   Now this reeks of the spirit of an enclosed community.   A secret that was all their own, shut
off like their own lives from the great world outside.   It
must have been an absolute and holy joy.   So we read :
'' Counsel having thus been taken, two brothers chosen for
the purpose carried it into effect.   For they took a little
wooden receptacle, fittingly prepared for this special purpose, and painted it inside, painting on the right-hand side
of the box '' S '' with a flourish, and on the left-hand side
'' D '' with a flourish, by which letters they meant to

[1] Lomax' Translation of De Antiquitate, p. 43.

indicate the name of St. Dunstan. Having therefore placed
the said relics in their receptacle, they hid them under a
stone sculptured for the purpose, in the great church,
nigh to the holy water, in the right part of the monks'
entrance, all others being entirely ignorant of the spot.
There he lay hidden, therefore, for 172 years." [1] Again,
those flourishes " have a most circumstantial and very true
ring about them. But according to the story, the Saint was
not to lie there for ever. The secret was to out. Here comes
a difficulty. The discovery was said to be made after a
great fire, apparently *the* great fire. This occurred in 1184,
which tallies with the 172 years from 1012, and so this part
of the story is later than William of Malmesbury, unless he
lived to be a very old man, and later than any edition which
he is known to have issued. Let me tell the story as recorded in " De Antiquitate Glastoniae." As time went
on, the secret was deposited with a brother called John
Canan, of "ripe age and most sagacious mind." " To the
care of this monk had been deputed a certain brother called
John de Watelege, young both in years and behaviour,
whom, on account of his natural good parts, the older man
treasured with exceeding affection." The monks, desiring
to learn the secret, stirred up this young brother to take
advantage of this affection, and learn it. Accordingly he
importuned the elder brother, who at length replied, " My
dearest son, before thou hast entered the Church, and art
about to sprinkle thyself with holy water, thou wilt touch
with thy feet the stone under which lieth hidden what thou
seekest. But ask no more about it ; think rather on what
thou hast heard in thy mind in silence." [2] But after John
Canan's death, John de Watelege proclaimed the secret.
This became common knowledge, but nothing was done.
At length came the great fire after " a considerable time
had elapsed." Canan and Watelege were apparently
dead. " The monks seeking some solace for their woes,
collected together what the flames had spared, especially
what was spared of the relics. At length, wondering about
St. Dunstan, there came back to their memory what John
Canan, and later John de Watelege had related—(as we
have described above)—and they debated the matter
together." [3] A few days later two brothers, Richard de
Cantone and Radulf Noc, went and explored, found the
stone, " and when they had turned it over, they espied
beneath it a little wooden compartment, strengthened on

---

[1] Lomax' Translation of De Antiquitate, pp. 45-6.
[2] Lomax' Translation of De Antiquitate, p. 47.
[3] Lomax' Translation of De Antiquitate, p. 48.

all sides by iron joints." [1]   The Prior and Convent were summoned. The case was opened. " They found therein the most sacred bones of the Blessed Dunstan, his ring also reposing on one of his finger bones ; and to untie the knot of doubt completely, they saw the painting within and the ' S ' with a flourish on the right side of the chest, and the ' D ' with its flourish on the left side, giving expression to the fact that St. Dunstan had been buried there." [2]   The monks " gathered them up with joy, and placed them in a shrine suitably covered with gold and silver, and with all seemly reverence and devotion, associating with them the shoulder and arm bones of St. Oswald, King and Martyr." There is the story. Whoever wrote, at any rate the latter part of it, it is a very natural story with certain evidences in its favour. Probably the dispute as to whether St. Dunstan lies at Glastonbury or Canterbury will never be settled to everybody's satisfaction. But whichever way we believe, Glastonbury is holy with memories of St. Dunstan, memories of the brilliant pupil, gifted artist, persecuted youth, visionary monk ; firm, generous, consecrated Abbot, far-seeing statesman and human man, tempering justice with mercy, and mercy with justice. Surely the most wonderful blend of startling gifts ! He stands in the very forefront of greatest Englishmen. [3]   And if the holy eventide of his life closed at that rival shrine of Canterbury, the centre of the Saxon as Glastonbury was of the Celtic Church his thoughts ever went back to the home of the morning and prime of his own life. To the last its sons attended him. Surely none would wish to rob us of this beautiful touch. And after all, what matter which has his body ? For both have his heart and his soul. Canterbury, beautiful Canterbury, can afford to be generous. Both shrines have been destroyed since Dunstan's day. Both rose again—Glastonbury to fall again. But Canterbury still stands proud and beautiful. And it pitieth all good men to see us in the dust. Surely once again St. Joseph's chapel will arise ? Not the rest of the Abbey ; it is not needed ; there is Wells. But as long as the Mother Church of Britain lies in ruins, all the daughters of

[1] Lomax' Translation of De Antiquitate, p. 49.
[2] Lomax' Translation of De Antiquitate, p. 49.
[3] It is impossible to deal properly with this great man in a sketch like this. The earliest life was written about A.D. 1000, just after his death, which Bishop Stubbs has edited for the Master of the Rolls series. E. W. Robertson discusses him in his " Historical Essays," Dean Hook in his " Lives of Archbishops," so does Mabillon, and Mr. Edmund Bishop in the " Dublin Review," Jan., 1885 (English Hagiology). William of Malmesbury, and Dean Armitage Robinson, his latest historian, are freely quoted above.

Britain must mourn.   But what avail tears when their
cause might cease ?   Perhaps Canterbury will be magnificently generous and help her fallen Mother to arise, if only
for the love of Dunstan !   Both monasteries have gone ;
both Churches remain.   May they have the true spirit of
the Churches !

ST. SIEGFRID, BISHOP OF NORWAY.

I am here putting down some notes that demand
further research.   This is the second additional saint that
I am including in this 2nd edition as probably connected
with Glastonbury—really the third, as, in my notes about
St. Thecla of Somerset, I have referred to St. Boniface,
shewing that he was at least in touch with Glaston.   It
was Miss Maria Conquist, a theological student at Upsala
University, Sweden, who first drew my attention to St.
Siegfrid.   She is trying to shew that Siegfrid, who converted her native Sweden, hailed from Glastonbury.   She
points out that William of Malmesbury, in a list of
celebrated Bishops connected with Glastonbury who were
Bishops in King Edgar's reign, includes Sigefrid, Bishop
of Norway, who died on the 5th April in a year not stated.
He had been a Glastonbury monk, and his love of his old
Alma Mater prompted him to send as a present four copes,
two with lions on them, and two yellow ones.[1]   Miss
Conquist says that Sweden had frequent communications
with England, and that Siegfrid, who christianized West
and South Sweden, had been in Norway.   He was an
Englishman.   He baptized the Swedish King Olaf about
1008.   The two links that caused her to make enquiries
of me were :—

    (1) The well where he baptized is called S. La
        Birgitta's ; that is, Bridget's or Bride's.   This
        is not after the Swedish St. Bridget, as the well
        was so called before she was born.   A Glaston-
        bury monk brought up amid the fields that St.
        Bridget had trodden, and where she was vener-
        ated in a chapel dedicated to her, where her bell,
        missal and other relics remained, and where (so
        great her repute) she was to be carved milking
        her cow, some two centuries and four centuries
        later, on the two most sacred sites—on the
        restored " Old Church," and on the Church on
        the Tor,—was likely to have called his holy
        christening well in the land of his successful

[1] p. 112, Lomax' edition.

labours after the sweet, lowly, mysterious saint
who had come as a visitor and a missionary to
his own homeland.

(2). St. Siegfrid's first bishop's-church or cathedral
in Sweden was dedicated to St. John the Baptist,
the dedication of the Parish Church of Glastonbury, a rare dedication in Sweden, possibly the
only one.

There is a question of dates. St. Siegfrid is said by
William of Malmesbury to have been Bishop in King
Edgar's reign. Edgar died in 975. As we have seen,
Siegfrid is said to have baptized the Swedish King about
1008. This date would fit in. Then comes the question
whether there was a Parish Church at Glastonbury dedicated to St. John the Baptist at that date. Most likely,
but not quite certainly. This church was originally the
Parish Church of All the Twelve Hides of Glastonbury,
for in Abbot Bere's Perambulations in 1507 and 1509 of
the Twelve Hides, the Vicar met him among the other
local magnates and is designated " Vicar of the Twelve
Hides of Glaston " in the former case, and " Vicar of the
Jurisdiction or Liberty [" Libertatis " is the word used]
of the Twelve Hides of Glaston " in the latter case.[1] True
that the church is not named in Domesday. Neither is
the Church on the Tor, which certainly existed. Only the
Great Abbey Church is named. After all, Domesday was
a tax book, and the Abbot owned practically everything.
Less than eighty years after Domesday, in 1143, Henry
of Blois, Abbot of Glastonbury, brother of King Stephen,
gets Pope Celestine's assent to making St. John's,
Glastonbury, contribute an annual sum to the Sacristy of
the Abbey.[2] And there are several other references to
the church about that period which suggest that it was
a well-established church by then. So that St. Dunstan
and St. Siegfrid may have worshipped in a church where
St. John's stands to-day. (There are traces of the Norman
Church in the present). So it does seem that the naming
of St. Bride's Well and St. John the Baptist's Cathedral
by Siegfrid in Sweden may very well have been a reminis-
cence of early days at Glastonbury.

The cult of St. John the Baptist was very strong at
Glastonbury. Not only was the great Parish Church dedicated to him, but there was a straight road from the south
porch of that church, through the former main gateway

[1] John of Glastonbury, Hearne's Edition, pp. 299 and 301.
[2] John of Glastonbury, Hearne's Edition, p. 184.

of the Abbey to the north porch of the Abbey Church. It was a straight line of about 200 yards. On the north side of that Abbey Church was a porticus or apsidal chapel dedicated to St. John the Baptist; and the Agnus Dei, the sign of St. John, was not only on buildings belonging to the Parish Church, but this emblem and that of St. John the Evangelist together are not infrequently found on buildings belonging to the Abbey.

What a wonderful missionary record was that of our great Celtic Church! Switzerland fell to Beatus, traditionally baptized in Britain by St. Barnabas. His cell, where he died in A.D. 96, is still shewn at Unterseen on Lac Thun. Mansuetus, an Irishman by birth, but converted and baptized in Britain, companion of St. Clement of Rome, the friend and pupil of St. John, founded the Church in Loraine and Illyria, being martyred in 110. Marcellus, of noble British birth, founded the princely Archbishopric of Treves, in early days often filled by Britons, dying, it is said, in A.D. 166. St. Cadval, another British missionary, founded in A.D. 170 the Church of Tarentum in Italy, the Cathedral of Tarento being dedicated to him. Patrick, Bride, Columba, Aidan, and an army of others. What names! Ireland, Scotland, Switzerland, parts of France and Italy, and more distant Illyria, all fell to their zeal. And then, when at length our heathen Saxon ancestors were converted, there is the same missionary and pilgrim zeal—Ina, Boniface, Thecla and Siegfrid of Sweden! And many another! What a galaxy! And the Mother Church of Britain, Glastonbury, was a home to them all. Of those named probably Aidan alone never trod her soil. If only all the blessed saints who have ever trodden the holy churchyard of Glaston could pass before us! But you have only to go there, and be still, and you feel their presence. May that holy spot never be neglected nor too much organized! It is easy to dispel a charm. Stonehenge, the Cheddar caves, and a thousand other spots have lost much of theirs. It is a sad day when silence does not conjure up long dead scenes, and the breeze does not suggest the rustle of a saint, and only to-day is present. That is death.

ABBOT RICHARD WHITING, MARTYR.

JUDICIALLY MURDERED 1539.

It is impossible to conclude this roll of some of the principal Saints of Glastonbury without some short account of Richard Whiting, that aged and sick man who sat in the

House of Lords as the second Mitred Abbot in the kingdom,[1]
and who was done to death by the greed and tyranny of a
monarch whose proper place was a convict prison, a scaffold,
or an asylum as a homicidal maniac.   Blessed Richard
Whiting, as he ought to be to our Church!   He was a
Somerset man of a family of gentle birth and moderate
possessions.   He had been Camerarius, or Chamberlain,
in his Abbey.   In 1524 Richard Bere, that active Abbot,
active in his travels, perambulations, and building proclivi-
ties, died.   He had begun the easternmost chapel of his
Abbey Church, the Edgar Chapel, which his successor
finished.   Everything seemed in the zenith of prosperity.
The monks of Glastonbury had a right to choose their Abbot
out of their own ranks.   Who was to succeed this great
prince?   For such was the Abbot of Glastonbury.   The
monks left it to no less a person than the great Cardinal
Wolsey to select which of their number should succeed,
and to nominate him.   The Cardinal's choice fell on
Richard Whiting on March 3rd, 1524, and him the monks
elected.   The motives of this choice, and the manner of
man Whiting was, are revealed to us by the language of
the mandate of induction addressed to two of the monks,
John Glastonbury and John Bennett: "A man of probity
and religion, far-seeing and discreet, commendable in life
morals and knowledge, circumspect in spiritual and temporal things, knowing and valuing the laws and liberties
of the said monastery."   And such he proved himself.   He
gave more attention to discipline and domestic things than
Abbot Bere did.   So excellent was his firm but kindly rule,
that even the King's Commissioners could find no weak
moral spot in the Abbey.   Dr. Richard Layton's own
report as Visitor remains.   Sending up some of the Holy
Thorn in flower, and various relics and their labels, he
ends with these words: "At Bruton and Glastonbury there
is nothing notable.   The brethren be so strict kept, they
cannot offend, but fain they would if they might, as they
confess; and so the fault is not in them.   Your most
assured poor priest, Richard Layton."   A most valuable
document!   Unwilling to give the monks any credit but
bound, to his honour, to say that he could find no fault!
Some commissioners, as we have reason to fear, were in
some places not so scrupulous.   They found what they
looked for, not what was there.   Doubtless in some cases

---

[1] Pope Adrian IV, Nicholas Brakespear, the only English Pope,
made St. Albans the first Abbey because he had been brought up there,
but in the minds of the Church and nation Glastonbury took precedence.
It was the most ancient, and in fact the greatest.

there was evil, as where not, and it was found! And Whiting's administration of the temporalities was as successful as his spiritual rule. The Abbey flourished. The King's Commissioners, Richard Pollard, Thomas Moyle, and Richard Layton, announcing the arrest of the Abbot, and their occupation of the Abbey, say : "We assure your Lordship it is the goodliest house of that sort that ever we have seen. We would that your Lordship would judge it a house mete for the King's Majesty, and no man else ; which is to our great comfort ; for we trust verily that there shall never come any double hood within that house again." The possessions of the Abbey were enormous. Practically the Abbot held sway over a belt of land twenty miles in width through the centre of Somerset. He had an income of at least about £30,000 a year in modern money. When he stirred abroad officially, 120 retainers, many of them esquires, accompanied him. All round Glastonbury he had pleasant manor houses, deer-parks, fish-ponds. Within the Twelve Hides he had power of life and death, and was supreme in matters temporal and spiritual. It was these things which caused the spoliation and destruction of the monasteries. The main-spring was political. Henry VII. had broken the power of the nobles. Henry VIII. broke the power of the Abbeys. A century later the people broke the power of the Crown. The political aim was enabled to get full movement because the pride of the Abbeys had led to insubordination against the Bishops— (the first real Dissenters of any note against the order of Christ's Church were the Abbeys ; the Church was divided against itself)—and because the monks had encrusted the Christian religion with superstitions which the light brought by the new learning and the re-discovery of the Bible through printing shewed in their true nature. Side by side with these faults were endless benevolences and lives of the greatest piety. The worst systems have always supporters better than themselves, and the best systems are always far above all their professors.

The psychical moment had come for institutions which had been at one time indispensable to drop into the background. A rule once necessary had now become to an awakening people oppressive. Now was the moment for jealousy and greed. The Abbeys were to reap the whirl-wind of their faults. They had lost much of their religious hold, and wherever there is firm rule there are sure to be some malcontents. "My Lord, I ensure you there were many bylls put up ageynst the Abbott by his tenaunts and others for wrongs and injuryes that he had done them," wrote J. Russell to the Lord Privy Seal, telling him of the poor old Abbot's trial and execution. Knowing what we do of this just, kindly old servant of God, we do not believe that these bills of complaint show any transgression of the code of the day. But behind these words is the unrest and rebellion of a populace against a system that is doomed. Wherever there is authority, there is always some discontent. And on the throne was a greedy, unscrupulous, instinctive criminal. And so the institutions which might have been mended were ended ; and in their place came the Poor Laws and their problems which we still have with us to-day.

There is a popular idea that Richard Whiting was a martyr because he refused to sign the Act of Royal Supremacy. This notion is very much fostered by the Roman Catholics. Nothing of the sort. There exists in the Chapter House of Westminster the Acknowledgment of the King's Supremacy, signed by Abbot Whiting and fifty-one of his monks. (There were forty-seven monks at the time of his election as Abbot.) The whole question of the King's Supremacy depends upon what interpretation is put upon the words used. It was no new claim. The moment the Roman Empire became Christian, its Emperors had a voice in the nomination of Bishops. In England in the Middle Ages there were not infrequent disputes between the Kings and the Popes on the same matter. It is not too much to say that the balance of power swayed according to the occupancy of the Throne or Papacy. When the King or Parliament were exceptionally strong, they frequently defied the Pope. So even did the Clergy occasionally in Convocation before the Reformation. When the Pope was a wonderful personality he frequently imposed his will. But it was a gradual usurpation. It was not natural to Britain. Neither the Roman Empire, nor the Roman Church, nor Feudalism ever had the complete hold in these islands that they held on the Continent. The Statutes of Provisors forbidding the suing for decisions in the Papal Courts, the Statute of Praemunire strengthening this, and making it treason to publish Papal Bulls in this country, and the Statutes of Mortmain to prevent the Church holding property, the evasion of which latter has given rise to the whole Court of Chancery and the Law of Trusts, are sufficient proof of these statements. These were all passed in the days of the Plantagenets. The Royal Supremacy in causes civil or ecclesiastical within the domain of England was not new, but it had never been so strongly defined, because the contention had never been so acute.

And to this day the Church accepts it " so far as the law of Christ permits." Even the Tudors had to be content with that reservation. And Glastonbury, like other religious houses, made the acknowledgment. It was not for this that brave old Richard Whiting died. He was done to death to strike terror into the hearts of lesser persons, much as the "finest buck in England," Henry's own uncle, the Duke of Buckingham, had been slain. If he did any technical wrong it was trying to hide from a sacrilegious robber things given to God. Henry wanted the Abbey, and just as he slew that lad, poor young Lord Dacre of the South (for being of a party that accidentally killed a keeper in an uproarious, sporting, poaching affray) because he wanted glorious Hurstmonceaux Castle,[1] so now Glastonbury Abbey is hunted to find excuses to brutally butcher this poor, frail old man. And pretexts were found. To quote the words of the Commissioners to the Lord Privy Seal, they "found in his study, secretly laid as well:

1. A written book of arguments against the divorce of his King's Majestie and the Lady Dowager.
2. A fair chalice of gold and divers other parcels of plate which the Abbot had hid secretly from all such Commissioners as have been there in time past."

This was written on September 22nd. He was arrested at his Manor of Sharpham. On the 14th November he was put to trial in Wells "for the robbing of Glastonbury Church"! He was condemned and executed on the 15th on the Tor Hill, Glastonbury, with two of his monks, being dragged to the Tor on a hurdle and hanged there. What a spectacle! His body was then beheaded and quartered, his head being stuck over the gateway of his Abbey, and the quarters of his body exposed at Wells, Bath, Ilchester, and Bridgwater, according to the barbarous custom of the times. So died the last of the prince Abbots of Glastonbury, a "most candid man, and my particular friend," as Leland called him, pious, generous, humble-minded, energetic, faithful in a humble capacity, and faithful as a ruler. Nothing could save him. In vain did he and his recognise the King as ruler of the kingdom, and the fount of justice. What a fount in this case! In vain did he receive the King's Commissioners with hospitality and respect. His doom was decreed. And because he would not violate his oath, abdicate his position and falsify his

---

[1] It was so Tudoresque, to strike terror into the hearts of the class that he wanted to break, and to please the populace by an appearance of justice, at one swoop. He, the cold-blooded rapacious executioner of poor defenceless wives!

trust, he was tried and put to death for "robbing Glastonbury Church"! His were not the head and quarters which should have adorned Somerset buildings for that offence.

There are two relics of the Abbot still in the neighbourhood. One is the chair in which he is said to have been tried at Wells. It is said to have been sent from the Abbey on purpose. If so, it was either the act of some loving retainer, or a revelation of the determination of his foes to emphasize his fall by trying him on his throne. For it is evidently a chair of state, and probably goes back into the dimmest antiquity. For it is exceedingly like a most ancient Celtic Abbot's chair of yew which the writer has seen, to which an amazingly distant date was ascribed. It stands in the long picture gallery in the Bishop's Palace at Wells. The other is a pall in the ancient Parish Church of St. John the Baptist, Glastonbury. Tradition says that it is made from a cope which Abbot Whiting wore in that Church. And expert opinion says that it is exactly of that period. It hangs in a case on the wall, and in the same case is a smaller piece of needlework of apparently the same date. Did his hand touch this, too? We are probably gazing at relics of this lovable and venerable martyr.

ST. GEORGE OF ENGLAND AT GLASTONBURY.

It is impossible to leave the question of the Saints of Glastonbury without any reference to St. George of England. It is also equally impossible to separate the legendary from the true. St. George must have been some great hero who travelled. Hence two of the greatest European States, England and Russia, claim him for their Patron Saint. And the legends tell of his travels. St. George is inextricably mixed up with Glastonbury. It is interesting to note that it is in his early days. So perhaps he was born an Englishman, though Cappadocia also claims him.

There was a Chapel of St. George in the Abbey. There is a Chapel of St. George in Glastonbury's glorious ancient Parish Church, St. John the Baptist. His arms, flanked by those of Courtenay, Earl of Devon, and Montague, Earl of Salisbury, are in the centre of a most beautiful, ancient chest in that Church, bought in the year 1421 to preserve the Parish accounts and deeds. About 100 years ago they were all found in it, sadly mildewed, and mixed up with other deeds and dirt. But thanks to

that chest and to St. George there still remain twenty-four
legible, precious, Churchwardens' accounts running back
to 1366, and many deeds, leases, etc., some of them going
back a century earlier.   St. George too is depicted killing
the dragon on a fragment of the parclose screen dated from
about 1350, which once separated St. George's Chapel (the
South transept) from the rest of the Church.   The obtru-
sive Puritans chopped down this, and the magnificent rood
screen,   fragments   of   which   also   remain.   But   the
parishioners are endeavouring to restore St. George's.   St.
George is also depicted on an ancient repoussé Nuremburg
alms-dish of latten belonging to the Parish Church, which
is said to date back to the early fourteenth century.   Mr.
Robert Neville Grenville, of Butleigh Court, near Glastonbury, possesses another.   And they may form part of a
set which once belonged to the Abbey, or more likely, the
Abbot.

The beautiful Pilgrim's Inn built by Abbot Selwood at
the end of the fifteenth century is the George Inn, and St.
George was once depicted killing the dragon as its sign.
A rent from this inn was once payable to the Parish Church.
Either this rent was charged on it, or the Pilgrims' Inn
belonged to the Parish Church, or was built on land belonging to it.   Possibly it replaced a building of Richard
Atwell's, who died in 1475, which may have formed part
of the property of his own building which he gave to the
Church.   One of the shields on the front of the Pilgrims'
Inn is an interesting proof that Glastonbury knew and
believed the legends of St. George when Abbot Selwood
erected the Inn about 1475.   The Arms of England, sur-
mounted by the Rising Sun of the House of York, are in
the centre.   To the right is the shield of St. George, the
blood-red cross on the white ground.   To the left is a blank
shield, which puzzles many people much because they do
not know the legends.   What a mercy that some wretch
has not filled it in with some fancy coat !   The English
legend is that St. George was born at Coventry, the son of
a nobleman called Albert, that his mother died in giving
him birth, and that in the grief that followed he was stolen
from the Castle unnoticed by one Kalyb, an enchantress.
George grew up in her charge.   When he came to man's
estate she gave him his horse Bayard, armour, and a shield,
but no device was upon the latter, because she did not wish
him to know whose child he was.   (Of course, this is an
abominable anachronism, as no coat was hereditary before
at any rate the reign of Richard I.)   There was no sword,
but she told him that he would find himself one.   This

latter he procured before he won a device for his shield.
In company with six knights whom he had delivered from
Kalyb's spell, he came to Avalon (or Glastonbury). One
of the treasures said to be kept at Avalon, besides the Holy
Thorn which grew from St. Joseph of Arimathea's staff,
was the sword " Meribah " with which St. Peter struck off
Malchus' ear in the Garden. This St. Joseph is said to have
brought with him to Britain. The pommel had been made
in Glaston, but the blade was claimed to be the veritable
blade. This sword was in the keeping of the Church of
Glaston. When the seven knights arrived the blank shield
of St. George drew attention. The Abbot was told of it,
and on the knights' arrival he hospitably entertained them.
If St. George was killed in the Diocletian persecution in
A.D. 303, as the Greek and Roman Churches say, there
was no Abbot at that date, for St. Patrick had not yet
gathered the Anchorites into the first monastery. But that
need not worry us. People tell stories badly. There may
well have been a primus among the Anchorites, if not de
jure, de facto. And such an one an ill-informed person,
after the all-powerful Abbots arose, would call " the
Abbot." We do not want to be robbed entirely of our
pretty legendary story, and its association with Avalon,
which has led to the blank shield standing as a silent and
unrecognised witness for centuries that Glaston accepted
this story. We do not like Goths in Glastonbury. They
should not tread our sacred soil. There are plenty of other
places for them, where they can breed like microbes in
glycerine. They will be just as happy there, and we
happier without them. We must call upon St. George to
deliver us.

Well, after supper the " Abbot " told them about the
sword Meribah, and how a wicked knight had sworn to get
hold of Meribah, and his consequent anxieties and fears.
(This sounds much more like the early Glaston Anchorites
living in huts, than a powerful, protected Abbey backed by
favouring kings.) Of course our St. George was chosen to
go against the knight, and of course he defeated him in the
presence of the other six knights. They rode at each other
full tilt with their spears seven times. At the seventh
encounter both were unhorsed, and St. George was
wounded under the left shoulder, and the blood gushed down
the length of his blank shield, and when he fell the blood
rushed across it sideways, and as he rose to fight with his
sword, the six knights saw the blood-red Cross of Christ
on his white shield, which St. George ever after bore.
Glaston's sword of Meribah soon did its work, and shivered

the other sword in pieces. The knight was at St. George's mercy. St. George was "a very perfect gentle-knight," as Chaucer would have called him, and he spared him. And Meribah was George's ever after.

The mediæval alms-dish already alluded to shews that while we in Glaston cherished our Glastonbury traditions of St. George, we were Catholic enough to hold the belief of the Saint's adventures in far Egypt. It is true that we are said not to have made the dish, but we at any rate accepted it and its story, for on it is depicted St. George killing the dragon, King Ptolemy and his wife looking out of a very distant window, Princess Sabra, kneeling, praying for her deliverer, while an angel floats sympathetically in the sky.

All legends! Yes, all legends, with doubtless some basis of truth and some early adventure in our Glastonbury and some later ones abroad. It is nice to know that not only our Saint was here, but his beautiful horse Bayard, and we are quite sure that the wonderful Glastonbury sword so delightfully reminiscent of King Arthur was an enormous help to him. Arthur's sword Excalibur was made at Glaston. We were evidently very clever craftsmen here before the day of St. Dunstan, who developed and consolidated our genius. Yes, it would be a great mistake to leave out this story of St. George as a baseless legend.[1] Since I began to write about it I feel much more sure of a delightful residuum of truth, covered over with the superstitions, and beliefs, and errors of centuries. But it is so nice to get the bit at the bottom. After all, there are things which some of us *know* which we can never convince others of. We have not the evidence. And you cannot give them an extra sense, if they have not got it.

But no wonder the mediæval boys and girls in Glaston believed in and loved St. George. They romped on his day, and they said their prayers in his chapel. And the elder people held him up as a beau ideal. There

[1] Every parent should spend quite a small sum and buy " St. George of England " by Basil Hood (Harrap and Co). for his child. In a beautiful new stained glass east window in St. George's Chapel, full of local saints, lately put up by Miss E. M. Bailey, of The Hall, Glastonbury, the main scene is St. George killing the dragon. The glass, which is of mediæval character, is by Messrs. Daniels and Fricker, of Kilburn, and well worth a visit. In the north window of the Sanctuary is 15th century glass, depicting among other things, a beautiful figure of the Virgin crowned, and St. Katherine, to whom the North Transept is dedicated. In the South there is 15th century glass, and even 13th century grisaille glass; the central figure is the native Saint, St. Dunstan, and the arms attributed by the Heralds to St. Joseph of Arimathea are shewn. It is regrettable that with all the scenes in St. Joseph's life available there is not a window to him.

were his empty shield and his full shield ever before them
on the great Pilgrims' Inn, and they knew what it all meant.
His full shield was on the chest protecting their Church
accounts, and the deeds of their property in the Church.
His story on the alms-basin did not inspire them as their
alms were offered, because alms were not offered in that
way in their day. But they gave their alms all the same,
and for St. George. The dry old Church accounts give
us peeps into the every-day life as well as the strictly
Church life of that day. And we learn that on St. George's
Day players came, and larger sums were reaped from the
play than on any other day. And poor old people had
alms distributed among them. In 1418 they restored their
Chapel of St. George, and the Suffragan Bishop came and
consecrated a new Altar there. There was a painted
banner of St. George in it. There was a relic of St. George
kept under lock and key. And there was an image of
George evidently on horseback set on high, but like everything else, it grew old. For in 1500 the horse required a new
tail, and one John Chyverton, a painter, re-gilded the
image, which must have been a large one, for he got paid
very highly for doing it, receiving no less than £6 13s. 4d.,
equal to about £60 in these days, if not more. Evidently
women and girls were taught especially to venerate St.
George, the deliverer of Princess Sabra, for the girls of the
Church subscribed £1 13s. 4d. towards this work, and the
women 13s. 4d., more than one-third of the whole cost.

No, no, no, if St. George belong to England—and what
Englishman would allow a foreigner to say that he did not?
—"St. George for England!" England owes him to
Coventry and Glastonbury. Coventry gave him birth:
Glastonbury armed him, and taught him to be a great and
good knight. Then the English wanderlust came on him
and, being what we made him, the rest of the world heard
of him.

THE MOST WONDERFUL TRADITION OF ALL

CHRIST AT GLASTONBURY.

Did Our Lord ever come to Glastonbury as a lad?
The story not only lingers here, but elsewhere. Briefly,
the tradition is this : That Our Lord accompanied St. Joseph
of Arimathea as a lad on one of the Saint's expeditions to
Britain to seek metal. For the possibilities of this legend,

and for the other legends and facts that fit in with it, I must quote my " *St. Joseph of Arimathea at Glastonbury*" (Third Edition, pp.17-18) :

" Perhaps there is some truth in the strange tradition which still lingers, not only among the hill folk of Somerset, but of Gloucestershire,[1] that St. Joseph of Arimathea came to Britain first as a metal merchant seeking tin from the Scillys and Cornwall, and lead, copper and other metals from the hills of Somerset, and that Our Lord Himself came with him as a boy. There is also a tradition in the West of Ireland that Our Lord came to Glastonbury as a boy.[2] The tradition is so startling that the first impulse is summarily to reject it as ridiculous. But certain it is that it is most persistent. And certain it is that amongst the old tin-workers, who have always observed a certain mystery in their rites, there was a moment when they ceased their work, and started singing a quaint song beginning ' Joseph was in the tin trade.'[3] Mr. Henry Jenner, F.S.A., late of the British Museum, narrates that some years back in North London during the making of tin sheets for organ pipes, before the molten metal was poured,[4] a man said every time, ' Joseph was in the tin trade.' And certain it is that if St. Joseph was a metal merchant he must somehow have got tin for bronze, and that Britain is almost the sole land for tin mines. And if he were a metal merchant, it is not inconsistent with his being a rich man. And the strange story of Our Lord's coming which is so very dear to simple Somerset hearts would be explained by the Eastern tradition that St. Joseph was the uncle of the Blessed Virgin Mary.[5] So if there be any truth in the ancient story, this old hill—" The Tor "—with its rites may have attracted the mart which first led here St. Joseph and the Redeemer before He began His ministry. And to it, after the wondrous Resurrection and Ascension, St. Joseph, laden with the New Message of the New Religion would wend his way on his mission from Gaul to Britain, the seat of Druidism. His knowledge of the Druids would account (in part) for his kindly reception by the Druids of France,

---

[1] The Ven. Walter Farrer, Archdeacon of Wells, told me that the legend is to be met with in Gloucestershire.

[2] The Rev. Canon A. R. B. Young, Prebendary of Clogher Cathedral in Ireland, has heard the tradition all his life.

[3] V. also Baring Gould's " Cornwall," p. 57.

[4] Quarterly Review of the Benedictines of Caldey, 1916, pp. 135-6.

[5] It is curious that King Arthur claimed descent from St. Joseph, and St. David, said to be his uncle, was said to be of kin to the Blessed Virgin Mary. For the descent of King Arthur from St. Joseph, see John of Glastonbury (Hearne's Edition), Vol. I., pp. 56-57 (small paper), where it is set out. He was 8th in descent.

and he would come to King Arviragus, or at any rate some of his subjects, as a not unknown person, and hence, perhaps, his kindly reception and the donation of land."

There is a tradition, too, at Marazion, in Cornwall, of St. Joseph coming there to trade with tin miners. Marazion means " bitter Zion." Its other name is still Market Jew. And it is a most ancient tradition that it was a colony of Jews who traded in tin. " Jews' houses," " Jews' tin," " Jews' leavings," " Jews' pieces," are still common terms in the Cornish tin mines. The oldest pits containing smelted tin are called " Jews' houses." [1]

William Blake, the poet (1757-1827), had evidently heard the tradition of Glastonbury, and embalmed it in beautiful verses, to which Hubert Parry wedded equally inspired music. With these I will end :—

JERUSALEM.

" And did those feet in ancient time
　" Walk upon England's mountains green ?
" And was the Holy Lamb of God
　" In England's pleasant pastures seen ?
" And did the Countenance Divine
　" Shine forth upon our clouded hills ?
" And was Jerusalem builded here
　" Among those dark Satanic mills ?

" Bring me my bow of burning gold !
　" Bring me my arrows of desire !
" Bring me my spear !　O clouds, unfold !
　" Bring me my Chariot of Fire !
" I will not cease from mental fight ;
　" Nor shall my sword sleep in my hand
" Till I have built Jerusalem
　" In England's green and pleasant land."

[1] V. Taylor's " Coming of the Saints," pp. 182-3. And v. also pp. 178-180 for the route of the tin merchants from Marseilles to Cornwall before Christ.

AFTERWORD TO THE FIRST EDITION.

To Strangers.

This is our Glastonbury. Do you not love her better now that you have heard her story—haltingly set forth? Is there another story like it in the kingdom?

To Glastonians.

What manner of persons ought we to be in all holy conversation, and in love and charity? Who is sufficient for these things?

AFTERWORD TO THE SECOND EDITION.

SOME EARLY EVIDENCES.

We are moved to write a slight outline of some of the earliest evidence for Glastonbury's story.

Eusebius, Bishop of Caesarea, born about A.D. 260, says : " The apostles passed beyond the ocean to the isles called the Britannic Isles (De Demonstratione Evangelii Lib. III). Eusebius was at the Council of Nicæa, A.D. 325, where also were the British Bishops of London, York and Caerleon.

Tertullian, born about A.D. 155, said : " Regions of Britain, which have never been penetrated by the Roman Arms, have received the religion of Christ." (Def. Fidei. p. 179.)

Origen, born about A.D. 185, in three different passages relates the conversion of Britain. (1) In Psalm cxlix ; (2) Homil. iv in Ezek. ; (3) Homil. vi in Luc, 1, 24.

Nennius, the first British historian, is full of laments at the decay of the Christian religion in Britain.

Gildas, born about A.D. 516, who died at Glastonbury, says Christ, the true Sun, afforded His light the knowledge of His precepts, to our island in the last year, *as we know,* of Tiberius Cæsar," *i.e.,* A.D. 37. (De excidio Britanniae, Sec. 8.)

Cardinal Baronius, the great historian and librarian of the Vatican, in his Ecclesiastical Annals, quotes an ancient Vatican MS., under the year A.D. 35, which states that in that year Joseph of Arimathea, Lazarus, Mary, Martha,

Marcella their maid, and Maximin a disciple were put by the Jews into a boat without sails and without oars, and floated down the Mediterranean to Marseilles, where they landed. This brings St. Joseph to France. Of course Marseilles is full of traditions and holy spots connected with the family of Bethany.

The Pseudo Gospel of Nicodemus, an Oriental MS. generally thought to be 4th century, but deemed by Tischendorf to be very early 2nd century, tells of St. Joseph suffering persecution.

Melchinus (Maelgwyn of Llandaff), said to have been uncle of St. David, and to have been "before Merlin," writing about A.D. 450, says : "Joseph of Arimathea, the noble decurion, entered his perpetual sleep with his xi companions in the Isle of Avalon, and lies in the southern angle of the bifurcated line of the Oratory of the Adorable Virgin. Moreover, he has with him two silver white vessels filled with the blood and sweat of the great prophet Jesus." This is the first definite linking of St. Joseph by name with Glastonbury.

St. Augustine, in his letters to Pope Gregory about A.D. 600 (quoted by the unknown Saxon Priest who wrote the life of St. Dunstan about A.D. 1000) says that "the first neophytes of Catholic law found in it (Glastonbury) a Church constructed by no human art, but by the hands of Christ Himself for the salvation of His people." A gross exaggeration which testifies to the claims and sanctity of the spot.

Isidore of Seville, who died A.D. 636, says that St. Philip preached Christianity in France, and "led barbarous nations, close neighbours of darkness, and bordering on the stormy ocean to the light of knowledge, and the haven of faith."

Freculphus, Bishop of Lisieux, A.D. 825-851, confirms that St. Philip preached and laboured in France.

William of Malmesbury, about 1129, in addition to his other works, wrote the first extant deliberate History of Glastonbury. He starts with the persecution of St. Stephen, which scattered abroad all the believers except the Apostles. He quotes Freculphus as saying that St. Philip preached in France. He says that St. Philip sent twelve missionaries to Britain led by his "dearest friend, Joseph of Arimathea, who buried the Lord." He states that the pagan King (Arviragus) and his two successors gave, and confirmed to them the xii Hides of Glaston ; that there, warned by a vision of the angel Gabriel, they built a Church, " fashioning its walls below circular-wise, of twisted twigs." It was dedicated to St. Mary, and he calls it " The Old Church," and says : "Glastonbury Church is therefore the most ancient in England that I know, and hence it gets its cognomen." He quotes written evidence of good credit found at St. Edmund's to this effect : 'The Church of Glastonbury did none other men's hands make, but actual disciples of Christ built it, being sent by St. Philip the Apostle, as was said before.' " William, the critical historian, possessing facilities which we have not, after his great works on the Kings and Bishops of the English, was asked to stay at Glastonbury on purpose to write its history, and became an adopted son of the house. What he wrote fits in with all the claims of Glastonbury from tradition and from written history. The more we study the evidence from all parts, the more remarkably it supports Britain's most ancient, unbroken story.

INDEX.

Page

Dubricius, St. 10, 32
Dunstan, St. 15, 16, 22, 30, 52—63, 72
Dunstan's Chapel, St. 53
   ,,   Psalter 16
Durham 51
Dyfan, Duvanus, or Deruvian, St.
           xi, 9—11, 15, 17, 26

E

Earl Marshall, The 37
East Anglican Chronicler xiv
Easter ... ... 24, 37—39, 44
Eastern Church 1, 6. 8
   ,, Saints 49
   ,, Tradition ... ... xiii, 74
East Pennard 18
Ecclesiastics, Statesmen 30, 56
Echfrid, Abbot 47
Edessa 12
Edgar, King 29, 53, 57, 62, 63
   ,, Chapel 65
Edgarley 53
Edgiva 56
Edington 46
Edmund I, King ... 52, 53, 55, 56
Edmund (Ironside) King 30, 58
Edmund's, St. ... ... xii, 4
Edred, King 56
Edward I, ...37—39
Edward III xiv
Edwin, King 44, 50
Edwy, King 56, 57
Egypt 72
Eleanor, Queen ... ... '37, 38, 41
Eleutherius, Pope ... xi, xii, 9—11
Elfan, St. ... ...10—11
Elijah, Prophet 56
Emerita, St. 11
England, xviii, 28, 39, 43, 62, 67, 69, 73, 75
   ,, unified 57
Escan Ceaster 48
Eschenbach. Wolfram von 41
Ethelbert, King 44
Ethelbricht, Brother 58
Ethelburga, Queen ... 43, 44, 50
Ethelwold, St. 57
Eumer 44
Europe ... ... ix, 42, 56
Eusebius ... ... xv, 1
Excalibur (Caliburn) 32, 40, 72
Exeter 48, 54

F

Fagan (Phagan) ... xi, 9—11, 15, 17, 26
Farrer, The Ven. Walter 74
Ferramere 18
Feudalism 67
Flanders, Court of 41, 56
Forbes, Professor Russell 3
France (Gaul) xviii, 2, 3, 41, 64. 74
   ,, Church of ... ... 7—9
Freculphus ... ... xii, 3

G

Gabriel St. 4
Galilee. The xvi
Gall. St. 24, 29
Gartom 22
Gauls xii
Geoffrey of Monmouth xi, 10, 11, 25
               30, 32, 33, 39
George. St. ... ... 29, 69—73
George's, St., Alms-dish 70, 72
   ,,   ,, Altar 73
   ,,   ,, Arms 70, 71
   ,,   ,, Chapel 69, 72, 73
   ,,   ,, Day ... ... '73

Page

George's, St., Dragon 70, 72
   ,,   ,, Horse, Bayard ... 70, 72
   ,,   ,, Image 73
   ,,   ,, Parentage 70
   ,,   ,, Relics 73
   ,,   ,, Screen 70
George Inn 70
George III. 28
George IV. 28
Germanus, St 14, 42, 50
Germany 47, 49
Gethsemane 71
Ghent 56
Gildas, St. ...
   xv, xvii, 2, 10, 11, 21, 32, 42, 43, 49
Giraldus Cambrensis ... 21, 36, 37, 39
Glamorganshire 42, 50
Glass Windows, Ancient 72
Glastonbury, ix—xviii, 1—32, 35, 37, 39—43,
      47—59, 61—66, 68—75
   ,, Abbey, xiii—xvi, 3, 5, 11, 12,
        15, 17—19, 21, 22, 26,
        30, 32, 35—37. 43,
        52—55, 57—66, 68, 70,
        71.
   ,,   ,, Library ... 33
   ,,   ,, Trustees xv—xvii
   ,, Abbots of 12, 17—19, 28, 35,
        36, 38, 45, 47, 49,
        51, 53, 55, 63—71
   ,, Arms of 32
   ,, Calendar 16, 22, 43, 44, 52
   ,, Charters ... 44—46,52
   ,, Church of xii, 4, 27, 45—47,
        68, 69, 71
Glastonbury Churches—
Benignus, St. (St. Benedict's) ... 5, 18
David's, St. 26
Dunstan's Chapel, St. 53
Edgar Chapel 65
Mary's, St. (St. Joseph's, The Old
   Church, The Wattle Church, etc)—
   xii, xvi. 2, 4, 6. 11. 14. 17. 21. 23.
   25, 28, 29, 34, 36, 42—44, 52, 67
Michael's. St. ... 17. 18, 21, 62, 63
Parish Church (St. John Baptist)
        18, 69, 70, 73
Patrick's Chapel, St. 15. 21
Peter and Paul, SS. 44
Glastonbury Churchwardens' Accounts
        70—73
   ,, John 65
   ,, Jurisdiction of ... 46
   ,, Monks 3. 62, 65. 67
   ,, Parish Church xiii. xiv. 18,
        63—70. 72
   ,, Tor 17. 21, 35, 40, 50, 68. 74
   ,, Traditions ... ix, xiii. 72
   ,, Saints 43
   ,, Vicarage 5
Gloucester, Robert Duke of xi, 10. 33
Gloucestershire 5, 74
Godney 46
Goode. William ... ... xiv, xvi
Gospel Oak 8
Gould. Mr. R. T. 48
Grael, Contes del 41
Greek Church 6, 71
Grenville, Mr. R. Neville 70
Grison Canton 12
Guienne 41
Guinevere, Queen ... 32. 34, 36—39

H

Haddan and Stubbs 25
Hades 35
Haleca, Bishop 6

Other books published by Research into Lost
Knowledge Organisation Trust